STEELE'S SCOUTS

Samuel Benfield Steele
and the North-West Rebellion

Wayne Brown

Heritage
House

National Library of Canada cataloguing in publication data

Brown, Wayne F., 1941-
   Steele's scouts

   Includes index.
   ISBN 1-894384-14-8

   1. Steele, Samuel Benfield, Sir, 1849–1919. 2. Riel Rebellion, 1885.
3. North West Mounted Police (Canada)—Biography. I. Title.
FC3216.3.S77B76 2001   971.2'02'092   C2001-910495-2
F1060.9.B78 2001

First edition 2001

Heritage House acknowledges the financial support of the Government
of Canada through the Book Publishing Industry Development Program
(BPIDP) for our publishing activities. Heritage House also acknowledges
the support of the British Columbia Arts Council.

Cover and book design by Darlene Nickull
Edited by Terri Elderton
Maps by Tom Howell

HERITAGE HOUSE PUBLISHING COMPANY LTD.
Unit #108 - 17665 66 A Ave., Surrey, B.C. V3S 2A7

Printed in Canada

The Canada Council | Le Conseil des Arts
for the Arts | du Canada

Canada

ACKNOWLEDGEMENTS

Historical books, like many projects one undertakes, can rarely be completed without relying on extensive resources. In my case I'm indebted to innumerable individuals who set aside their valuable time to provide information that I desired. Some work in the historic field as an occupation, yet others have lent assistance for the pure love of history and the desire to understand our past.

Above all I wish to express my sincere appreciation for the funding I received from the Alberta Historical Resources Foundation. Their financial assistance made it possible to complete this book within a reasonable time. When I initiated the project I had little concept of the costs involved and the Foundation's assistance was a virtual godsend. To its coordinator, Ms. Monika McNabb, I especially extend my appreciation for her guidance.

Other acknowledgements are to the people I consider "my friends," who have unselfishly shared their knowledge of the late 1800s, hoping that it won't become lost. I hesitate to even start naming individuals for fear of missing someone who may be most important, so to them I apologize for my mental lapse—and thank them profusely.

The first has to be my dear old friend, Pete Holt, an historically aware farmer who lived in the area around Fort Pitt in the early 1900s. His shack was next to the remnants of Constable Cowan's exhumed grave above the old fort site, and it was his superb memory that laid the groundwork for this work. Second is another, equally respected gentleman, Edgar Mapletoff, who likewise lived in the area about the same time. He was familiar with many of the sites that are not marked and could specifically identify their exact locations. Inevitably, my investigation would later confirm his accuracy.

To Eugene Makokis I'd like to extend my appreciation for the introduction to residents of both Saddle Lake and Whitefish Lake Indian Reserves and the folklore that supplemented written accounts of 1885. It's so unfortunate their ancestors have been branded by past accounts of the uprising when in fact they were acts of absolute desperation that any one of us may have resorted to had we been in their circumstances. To them, "Hey, hey winakona!"

Over the last few years I've grown to know two men who are incredibly knowledgeable about this time frame in Western Canadian history: Keith Davidson and Rusty Williams of the Lloydminster area. Keith is a local writer who specializes in "History Mysteries," which are highly appreciated in the region. He is a superb storyteller with a mind-bank that is nothing short of phenomenal. Rusty, Keith's side-kick, is unreal at deducing site locations and probable important points, simply by reasoning and not using one of those metal detector "gadgets."

On the professional side my first thank-you must go to those outstanding employees of the Glenbow Archives in Calgary. Their patience has to be "far above and beyond the call" to endure my bungling ineptness; yet time and again, they came to my assistance with what was required, and a smile. Likewise I'm indebted to the Alberta and Saskatchewan Provincial Archives staff, as well as those at the City of Edmonton Archives who furnished far more details than I could have expected. Other invaluable sources were the RCMP historians and Archives in Ottawa along with William MacKay, curator of the RCMP museum at Depot in Regina. Also my indebtedness extends to Donald Klancher for his unexpected help in resolving some final police related details and for the photographs he unselfishly provided.

In saving the most important for last I'm indebted to my wife Marilyn, not only for her patience, but for sharing and often enduring many of our field adventures with me simply because she too loves to learn more about our cherished heritage.

Wayne F. Brown
Paradise Hill, Saskatchewan

CONTENTS

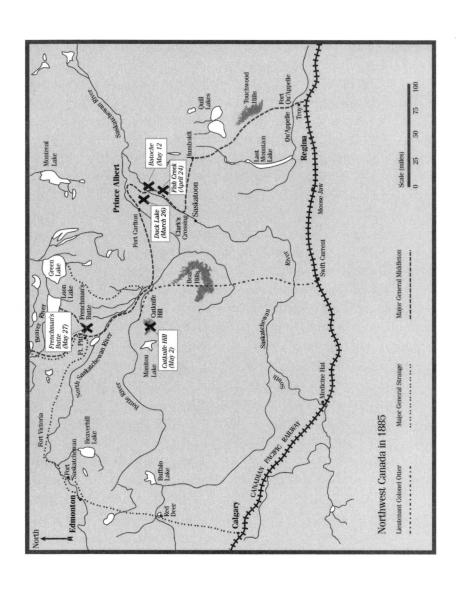

Northwest Canada in 1885

Lieutenant Colonel Otter	··········
Major General Strange	·········
Major General Middleton	‒ ‒ ‒ ‒ ‒

Scale (miles)

0   25   50   75   100

FOREWORD

The federal government in Ottawa had ignored the deplorable plight of the Indian and Métis people of the western prairies for over twenty years, and now it faced a full-blown rebellion as a result of its inept negligence. The Métis, with Louis Riel as their leader, had formed a provisional government at Batoche. The Cree Indians, led by War Chief Wandering Spirit, had murdered nine white settlers and taken an undetermined number of hostages at Frog Lake. The unrest was spreading like a plague and it appeared the entire Canadian west was about to erupt into a full-scale war.

Ottawa quickly marshalled military forces to regain order. General Frederick Middleton was placed in overall command, and a three-pronged military response was developed. One force, led by Middleton himself, would march on the Métis at Batoche, Colonel William Otter would march to and hold Fort Battleford, while the third, led by General Thomas "Jingo" Strange, would deal with the Indians at Frog Lake. Strange's force, by the nature of its mobility, could not succeed without an elite scout group as its "eyes." Strange knew that no one was more qualified to command it than North West Mounted Policeman, Samuel Benfield Steele.

Sam Steele is a unique character in Canadian history. He was born in Canada and as a young militia soldier at the time of Confederation served in the force that quelled the first Métis uprising in 1869 at the Red River Settlement. He was third to join the new North West Mounted Police and endure the "March West" in 1874; and he then witnessed the signing ceremonies of Indian Treaty Number Six (also known as the Fort Carlton-Fort Pitt Treaty). In just over a decade of service Sam had seen vast changes in the west, from the days of immense free-ranging herds of buffalo to the coming of the railway, which triggered a constant flow of settlers and development on the prairies. He could see that change was unavoidable, but he did not believe that violence as a solution to the inevitable problems those changes brought should be a part of the new west.

For General Strange to employ a Mounted Policeman was natural. And there wasn't anyone more aggressive, more tenacious, or more confident than Sam Steele. During his eleven years of experience as a policeman in the west, he had developed the reputation of "trouble-shooter" for the force. He knew the prairies and he knew the strength of the Cree warriors. This campaign against Wandering Spirit and his rebels would test the mettle of every man in the Alberta Field Force— and in particular Steele's Scouts—to the limit. Only the best could turn the threat of a full-scale rebellion into a last gasp of a disappearing territorial frontier.

PROLOGUE

Canada's first major industry—the fur trade—evolved through the actions of two rival companies. The oldest was the Hudson's Bay Company (HBC), which had established its original fur-trading posts on the large northern bay bearing the same name. Over a century later in 1804 the North West Company, an amalgamation of several small, independent trading companies, began expanding aggressively by going inland to the trappers unlike the HBC, which preferred compelling the trapper to come to its forts. This new business threat pressured the HBC into building additional posts at Rocky Mountain House, Fort Edmonton, Fort Carlton, and a few other locations sprinkled across the west. The expansion of these companies' trading brought more and more men of European ancestry to the northwestern part of the continent.

In the late 1700s and early 1800s the trading post "factor" or chief trader in charge, possessed significant power despite company policy not to become involved in local disputes, wars, or uprisings. The post's intention was to be neutral territory where trade with anyone could take place. Contrary to policy, many of the HBC factors did act as judge or mediator in disputes, whenever it was to the benefit of the company. There was no point in losing one or both trappers in a deadly fight when mediation would ensure continued business from both parties. But eventually settlement and the coming of the North West Mounted Police reduced the factor's status and power to nothing more than that of a storekeeper.

During the 1800s the term Métis referred to a person of North American Indian and French or English parentage, most often the descendant of a French voyageur, fur trader, or trapper who took an

Indian woman as his "wife." To the Frenchman this union was often a necessity for his success in dealing with Indians; even his physical survival depended on her company if he were to keep his scalp and see the dawning of the next day. The Métis were often called "half-breeds" without implying a negative ethnic reference. Today the term "half-breed" is considered derogatory in nature, and the definition of a Métis person has been further clarified to be those "belonging to or descended from the people who established themselves in the Red, Assiniboine and Saskatchewan River valleys during the nineteenth century, forming a cultural group distinct from both Europeans and Indians."[1]

As the Métis colonies spread westward, one of the more prominent settlements became St. Boniface, near today's Winnipeg along the banks of the Red River. The land was laid out in the traditional way of the French seigneurs: in long, narrow strips, running back from the water. This style of land division afforded each landowner access to the river and transportation, essential to financial survival. Very few of these parcels of land were titled; that is, officially recorded and registered on paper.

As the English government extended its authority westward from Ottawa, it also began to survey the land. The English system of surveying was in a block form of sections and townships as we see today on our modern maps. This kind of land division was a necessity to establish property access in an organized way, envisioning roads, farms, and towns far removed from the rivers. With surveying came the paperwork: registration of land, titles, or deeds to the land for each owner. Obviously this conflicted with the Métis' method. Since the Métis' political representation was very limited and often ignored due to their smaller population, they rarely received fair representation in the government. It frustrated them immensely.

In the Red River Settlement, the Catholic church had encouraged and promoted conversion of the Métis to agriculture from the traditional hunting-based livelihood of the past. Some of the youth were given a better than fundamental education through the church. One of these promising young men was Louis Riel, born on October 22, 1844 in the Red River Settlement. His grandmother, Marie-Anne Lagimodiére, a strikingly beautiful and competent woman, held the distinction of being the first white woman to live in the northwest. In a true pioneering spirit she spent nearly three years at Fort Edmonton from 1808 to 1811, acquiring the utmost respect from Indian and white alike.

Not long after Louis Riel's birth, Samuel Benfield Steele was born January 5, 1849, in rural Ontario. His father Elmes Steele, a retired British Naval Captain, had already raised a family in Europe before emigrating to Canada at age 51 with his wife and their six children. His wife died in the early 1840s and Elmes re-married in 1848. Sam was the first child born of this second marriage, which produced six children, four boys and two girls.

Sam was a woodsman from the first, wandering the forests, glens, and marshes, learning the skills of the bush that were to support him in the future. He acquired his initial schooling from a library of books his father had brought from Europe and later attended a private school in Orillia, Ontario. The schoolmaster's wife gave Sam an acceptable capability in the French language at the same time as he achieved top of the class marks in school. Sam's father died in 1865, so for a few years he lived with his half brother, John, who taught him riding, musketry and other skills he'd depend on in the future. The heavy, unwieldy, muzzle-loading rifles and shotguns were cantankerous firearms that required more than ordinary capability for the shooter to become a marksman, yet Sam proved a natural. The style of riding he learned was the English military way, back erect with the chin pulled in; no "cowboy slouch" was tolerated in the Steele family.

Sam began service in the militia at the time of the Fenian raids into Canada.[2] He claimed he joined the militia at "about sixteen" years of age. Sam didn't see any action, but as a member of the 6th Company of the 35th Leicestershire Regiment, he excelled in the officer training courses. Typical of Steele's nature he scored 100 percent in drill and discipline.

Louis Riel's life was uneventfully normal for a Métis boy until he began attending school. His Catholic priest teachers encouraged him as he developed his ability to convincingly express his point of view. In his mid-twenties the young eloquent Métis gained his first political experience when the Hudson's Bay Company transferred its ownership of company land back to Canada in 1869. A substantial quantity of land around the Red River Settlement was involved in the terms enacted under the Manitoba Act, which at the same time incorporated Manitoba as a province. These negotiations took place in England without any Métis consultation; so, the disgruntled Métis established a provisional government with John Bruce elected as president and Louis Riel as secretary. Over the ensuing weeks, Riel, the better educated and more articulate of the two, came to dominate their assembly.

In 1869, the Métis under Riel presented a disturbing situation in the Red River Settlement near Lower Fort Garry (about 45 kilometres northeast of present day Winnipeg). The Red River Rebellion, as it became known, reached its climax when Riel, in the name of the Métis provisional government, orchestrated the execution of Thomas Scott. Scott was a loudmouthed, obnoxious Orangeman who frustrated Riel at every turn. He was arrested, expediently tried for treason, then dragged out to the east gate of Fort Garry and shot by a firing squad.

To say the news of this execution caused a furor in Ottawa would be an understatement! The authority of Canada, and more importantly, "The Queen," had been tested; the Métis must be repressed quickly and convincingly. A military response was the necessary action. The man chosen for the task was Colonel Garnet Wolseley who, with years of militia experience, was popular with everyone in Canada and had the capability to deal effectively with "that political upstart, Riel!"

Wolseley began assembling his force, and Steele volunteered immediately. Despite his previous experience and officer schooling he chose to serve as a private, keeping his full qualifications to himself. He wanted to experience the trials of the lower ranks, something he would never know if appointed as officer. The trip west to Fort Garry was difficult for the force and physically punishing for the men. Steele used his fitness to advantage and at the portages would shoulder two hundred pounds of pork or armament in addition to his own 70-pound pack. Each York boat of the brigade carried about four thousand pounds of cargo on board. The boat and supplies were unloaded at each portage and the boat skidded over corduroy (crosswise lying logs) from one shore to the next waterway to be reloaded so the trip could resume.

On August 29, 1870 the force reached Fort Garry to the cheering of jubilant settlers lining the banks of the river. Nowhere to be found were the rebellious Métis, their provisional government, or Louis Riel. Like "will-o-the-wisps" they had melted into the countryside, Riel himself slipping into the United States. The bulk of Colonel Wolseley's force was soon recalled back east, but Steele was able to manipulate his way into remaining as a part of a small occupation force that was to serve as a deterrent against further Fenian raids.

Sam's service at Fort Garry gave him his first exposure to "The West." He loved the way of life, the mixed culture of the Métis, with their dress, and the stories of their experiences on the plains. Sam not only listened, but he actually took notes in a diary, which he kept—as a good military officer would—for his entire life. In it he also recounted his first observation of the catastrophic effects made by smallpox on the Indians as the epidemic raged uncontrolled through their families. Their helplessness saddened him.

While he was at Fort Garry an election was held to fill the seats of the Legislative Assembly for the new province of Manitoba. The political campaigns were run in a wild, uncontrolled manner with copious amounts of liquor supplied to anyone who promised his vote to the candidates. Gang tactics, intimidation, bribery, and fisticuffs were common. The unhealed political wounds of the Red River Rebellion were still evident. Captain Villiers and his Quebec Rifles, a mounted militia, assumed a policing role to keep the election from degenerating into anarchy. Villiers employed a judicious use of force in trying to deal fairly with each situation as it arose, and thereby he gained the confidence of all sides in the election. The lesson was not lost on Steele, who recognized just how effectively level-headed police work defused hostile situations.

In the spring of 1871, Steele's unit was disbanded and he found himself back at Fort Henry in Kingston, soon becoming a member of the Royal Canadian Artillery, the first permanent militia in Canada. He was joined by his younger brother Richard under the command of an ex-member of the Royal Irish Constabulary, Lieutenant Colonel George A. French. Sam upgraded his military qualifications with artillery courses and was promoted to the rank of sergeant in "A" Battery. He was next appointed as an instructor to a French-speaking troop from Quebec. Military life for Sam was everything he desired amongst his troop mates: doing their daily duties, and in the evening at the barracks, telling stories, and sharing a few cups of rum. The daily discipline and regimentation in uniform supplied a feeling of pride that suited him perfectly.

The Red River Rebellion had helped the Métis to finally receive some recognition from the Canadian government. When Manitoba became a province of Canada on July 15, 1870, most of the terms were a result of Riel's negotiations with Ottawa. But the new province was a part of the dominion of Canada, and as such, would require a policing force that demonstrated the country's sovereignty over the sparsely populated land.

The Métis would not have the province to themselves. In the years that followed many Métis families quietly packed what they owned into carts and drifted westward to new settlements, such as Batoche and St. Anne, to make a fresh start. The land they left was reclaimed by the federal government and redistributed to English settlers. The Red River Rebellion may have been squashed, but the angry feelings of the rebellious Métis were not.

Chapter 1

STORM CLOUDS OF A REBELLION

In 1871, when news of the smallpox epidemic, the liquor trade to the Indians, and general lawlessness of the territories reached Ottawa, it caused major concern within the government. Military officer Lieutenant William Francis Butler, dispatched to assess the unrest in the territories, went from Winnipeg to Fort Edmonton and Rocky Mountain House and returned by a more southern route along the South Saskatchewan River, gauging the situation. He travelled about five thousand kilometres in 119 days by horse, dog team, and on foot. On his return he submitted a report to the Manitoba governor, outlining the reasons for the lawlessness, the approximate Indian population, the status of the smallpox epidemic, and other details. He recommended the formation of a police force to bring order to the chaos out west.

Prime Minister Sir John A. Macdonald who had long dreamed of uniting Canada by building a railway, and who also worried—correctly—about the possibility of the United States occupying the western plains (an idea Louis Riel had strongly promoted while he was living in the U.S.), felt the surest way to demonstrate Canadian sovereignty was by sending a policing force out west. An enabling act for the North West Mounted Police was passed on May 23, 1873.

Then on June 1, 1873 some white wolf hunters massacred 36 Assiniboine near Abe Farwell's Trading Post in the Cyprus Hills. When this news reached Ottawa in August, Macdonald put his police legislation into action.

Abe Farwell's Trading Post, Cyprus Hills
*Scene of an Indian massacre by white wolf hunters on June 1, 1873
precipitating the formation of the North West Mounted Police. A year
later the NWMP marched west, spreading law and order as they went.
The trail in the foreground is the Old Fort Benton trail.*

In the spring of 1873 Sam Steele heard the rumours of a mounted
force being created for service in the territories. By September 25, 1873
Major James Walsh, a former commander of a cavalry troop, was
appointed as sub-inspector and began recruiting suitable candidates, so
Steele went to see Walsh. After a brief interview he was offered the position
of major in the new force provided he could obtain his release from his
duties at Kingston. Steele rushed back to his commanding officer, only
taking time to pick up his two brothers, Richard and Godfrey, as well as
two other friends on the way. Colonel French, in the knowledge he was to
command the new force readily gave them their leave for he knew he
would need good reliable men in his new command.

Recommendations to Sir John A. Macdonald's government suggested
a mobile armed force of about five hundred and fifty men would be
required. It would be beneficial if they were dressed in red similar to
that of the militia who had impressed the Indians so much at Red River,
declaring that the "Great White Mother's men wear red coats and they
are our friends." A tunic similar to the British dragoons was chosen

Newspaper advertisement
Would you have applied?

(with gold braid being kept to a minimum), complemented by either a white helmet for dress or a small "pillbox" working hat.

In October the initial recruits, including Sam Steele, headed to Fort Garry for preparation and training. The men were all sworn in, "to well and faithfully, diligently and impartially execute and perform such duties as may from time to time be allotted." The first three to sign the regimental role were Arthur H. Griesbach, Percy R. Neale, and *Samuel Benfield Steele!*[3]

At Fort Garry, Steele became the recruits' nemesis on the parade square. He foot-drilled them hard, bellowing orders as he marched them in the traditional military formations. After foot drill came riding drill, then rifle and pistol training and practice. He built the training traditions of the force as he moulded the men. The picture of a modern Royal Canadian Mounted Police member on horseback is a reincarnation of Steele and his horsemanship. Many retired members of the force today, who trained with horses at Depot, remember being berated by the instructor if they fell off their horses. As a recruit lay prostrate the instructor demanded he make sure the horse wasn't injured and to "look after the poor thing." It's said this, too, was a legacy of Steele who had chastised his own brother for being awkward on his mount and getting thrown.

Steele had extra duties besides that of instructor, having to break and train the newly acquired horses. He fell back on some of the traditional cavalry practices, teaching them to be steady while the rider fired a rifle, to lie on the ground and provide a bulwark for a besieged member, and for both to work as a team. They worked hard at teaching the horse not to shy when startled; surprising the horse was a favourite tactic of the Indians when trying to intimidate a policeman in a confrontation. Because of his military background, his booming voice, and inexhaustible hardness, he acquired the nicknames "Smoothbore Steele" and "Simcoe Sam."

The only respite from outdoor training was when the thermometer fell below minus 36 degrees Fahrenheit. Reveille was at 6:30 a.m. after a night sleeping on wooden pallets supported by sawhorses (a practice not changed until about 1900). The recruits first looked to the horses, then had breakfast. Training lasted all day and supper was at 6:00 p.m. followed by laundry and uniform maintenance until lights out at 10:30 p.m. It was fortuitous the recruits were subjected to this type of rigid training as the next summer would test each of them to the limit. It seems Steele must have had a premonition of what they were to face.

The commencement of "The Great March" came on July 8, 1874, when at Colonel French's command the column of police moved out of Fort Dufferin (near today's Emerson) and headed westward. Traditionally the first day covered a very short distance to allow time for horses and men to recover from the inevitable "rodeo" and for them to determine what had been forgotten, what to discard as unnecessary, and to make a myriad of other adjustments. This column was unique in history because behind the divisions of scarlet-coated men came the inevitable supply wagons: a collection of farm machinery, cattle, oxen, and artillery guns.

As the march progressed it wasn't uncommon for the column to be spread over sixteen kilometres with stragglers extending even further beyond. On July 29, Inspector Jarvis was detailed by Colonel French to take the sick or injured men and livestock, along with a dozen fit members, and split off the main force. They were to head northward along the Red River cart trail to Fort Ellice, Fort Carlton, and eventually, to Fort Edmonton.

Sam Steele and his brothers, Dick and Godfrey, were part of this small group, shepherding the plodding animals along despite grave doubts about their chances of success. The condition of the horses was especially appalling because of their unwillingness to eat the wild grasses of the prairie. They were shadowed by Indians, fought a grasshopper plague, and nursed the livestock along, until they reached Fort Ellice, near the town of St. Lazare on the Manitoba-Saskatchewan border.

On September 11, they staggered into Fort Carlton, spent a week recuperating, and then forged on to Fort Pitt and finally Fort Edmonton. The worst of the trail proved to be the last one hundred kilometres with both men and animals collapsing in exhaustion from trudging through the knee-deep mud and continually sinking in the soft muskeg ground. On November 1, 1884 the remnants of the column drew on the little energy left and tried with their utmost to march proudly through the gates of Fort Edmonton.

After the traditional festivities of Christmas at Fort Edmonton, Steele and the other members began their enforcement of the illegal sale of liquor to the Indians. He participated in dog sled patrols in temperatures of minus 50 degrees, learning the techniques of severe cold survival.

When summer came, the *Northcote*—a Mississippi River type of paddlewheel steamboat—arrived on its first run upriver with Steele's notice of a promotion to sergeant major and a raise in pay to $1.25 per day along with a re-posting to Swan River in western Manitoba. He attended the signing of Treaty Number Six at Fort Carlton in 1876 and listened to Peter Erasmus interpret the agreed-upon conditions to the assembled bands of Cree. They were well aware of their plight with the decimation of the buffalo, and these treaties—although not really a "good deal"—appeared to be the only alternative to starvation. The government party then marched to Fort Pitt, north of present-day Lloydminster, where the process was repeated at a co-signing there. At this ceremony Steele watched as the chiefs of each band signed the treaty. One chief known as Big Bear from the Frog Lake area ominously stalled, then declined!

Steele was next transferred to Fort Macleod in the Alberta territory, not far from the United States boundary. The next few years he was very busy keeping the district peaceful, being constantly tested by whisky traders and Indians, whose culture made horse stealing a socially acceptable practice. After Custer's annihilation by Chief Sitting Bull's warriors at Little Big Horn, the entire Sioux Nation began to filter into Canada, seeking a refuge from the "long knives" (as they called the American cavalry). Although the situation remained tense, Sitting Bull kept his word and there was little real trouble all the while they remained in the country. Steele participated in the organized departure of Sitting Bull back to the United States in July 1881. He had an opportunity to meet with U.S. cavalry officers at the border and make a comparison. He was especially impressed with the way the Americans were equipped. They had good tents, stoves, bedding, food, and firearms whereas the NWMP were expected to make do with antiquated firearms, just a few blankets, and a campfire for cooking—even in the dead of winter.

Sam was able to return home to Simcoe county in Ontario in 1882 for his first leave since he had been sworn in. He was now 31 years old,

Sam Steele and Fellow Officers Fort Walsh, 1880.
Dr. G. Kennedy (left), Sam Steele (seated centre), Lief Crozier
(standing), Francis Dickens (seated right), and John Cotton
(reclining). Crozier's defeat at Duck Lake on March 26, 1895 and
Dickens' abandonment of Fort Pitt to the Indians on April 15, 1885,
rank as low moments in NWMP history. Cotton, the Officer-In-Charge
of Fort Macleod during the rebellion, saw no direct action.

a seasoned veteran of the western plains, and full of stories about his adventures. His relatives sat in awe listening to him tell of Indians like Sitting Bull, of shady saloonkeepers such as Kamoose Taylor who ran the Fort Macleod Hotel, and of strong-willed Mounties of James Walsh's stature. Typical of Sam, any adversity he experienced was conveniently forgotten or bypassed with a joke. Even in his autobiography he characteristically dwells little on his hardships. Off duty Sam was a very likeable man despite never losing his aura of authority and his belief in "spit and polish." He was always immaculate in his dress, displaying a well-trimmed moustache—a common feature amongst policemen, even to this day. After supper he liked to adjourn to the porch, smoke his pipe, drink a glass of rum, record the day's events in his diary, and contemplate as the sun set.

When Sam returned to duty, it was along the Canadian Pacific Railway (CPR) rail line as the steel stretched westward over the grassy plains.

Most of his work was liquor control among the rail workers for the CPR. Dealing with the ever-present danger of prairie fires, which could rage across the wind-blown prairie faster than a man could run, was also important work. Anyone caught setting a prairie fire received little sympathy from all policemen, not just Steele. Sam was also directed to establish a new post on the railway in the territory of Assiniboia. He selected a suitable location near where collected buffalo bones were dumped beside the track for shipment back east. He named a picturesque creek nearby "Wascana," an Indian word meaning "pile of bones." After the planning and laying out of a police post—the predecessor of the RCMP's Training

Samuel Benfield Steele
A young Sam Steele in formal dress uniform about the time of Treaty Number Six signing.

Depot—construction commenced, and the city of Regina eventually grew up nearby. The railway crew continued pushing westward into the territory of the Blackfoot Nation on their way to the Pacific.

In 1883 he assumed command of the Calgary district and continued his work with Indians, curtailing their persistent horse stealing habits. Near the Indian reserve at Gleichen he met retired military officer Major General Thomas Strange. This tall, bearded, monocle-wearing Englishman ran one of the largest ranches in the territories—the Military Colonization Company. Strange was having a constant problem with livestock theft because of his proximity to the reserve. On one occasion Steele rode out to the ranch at Strange's request. The two men found they got on well together because of their similar backgrounds, and they went to the reserve to brazenly lecture the chief about horse stealing.

Several days later one of Steele's sergeants, William Fury, became involved in a futile attempt to arrest an Indian—Whitecap—for horse theft from the Colonization ranch. Despite Fury's reputation for courage in adversity, Whitecap eluded him and was eventually tracked down and apprehended in Calgary. These three aptly named men—Strange, Steele, and Fury—would converge again in the near future.

Louis Riel, after becoming a member of parliament, was finally expelled from his seat in the federal government. In 1876, because of his mental instability, he was quietly committed to the St. Michel-Archand Asylum near Montreal, Quebec. Just short of two years later he was released; he slipped into the United States and found his way to Montana in the fall of 1879. He eventually acquired a teaching position at St. Peter's Mission, just outside of today's Great Falls, Montana, to unknowingly await the call to return and "save" the Métis at Batoche.

The Métis, resettled from the Red River, faced the same bleak future as the Indian nations. The buffalo were gone and with them the traditional way of life, living by what they hunted. In 1883 the open market in St. Paul, Minnesota had processed through its doors 150,000 hides. *The very next year*, the same in which Riel returned to Canada, the number plummeted to a meagre *300 skins*! The Indians at least had land set aside for them in the form of reserves, and received a little help promised by the treaties, but the Métis had nothing! The government continued to ignore them and their demands—the same as those made more than ten years previously—for recognition of land ownership, the negation of government land surveying, and of course, representation in government.

There appeared to be no headway in resolving any of these concerns and with the disillusionment and anger running high, a village meeting was held in Batoche. Some attendees advocated "oiling the cannon" there and then and others suggested the government would eventually offer solutions if they were patient. However, a consensus emerged among the participants present: Louis Riel had to be convinced to return and lead them in gaining government recognition and a resolution to the situation. Gabriel Dumont and two other men were delegated to ride for Montana and persuade Riel to return. Riel was easily convinced to uproot his family and journey to their new home of Batoche, in the territory of Saskatchewan. The boost to his ego was significant, supporting his conviction that he was indeed the "Métis' Saviour."

At Batoche, Riel began at once to draw people to him. A meeting in Prince Albert went very well and he gained strong local support, due to his "low-key" approach. He also tried to entice the Indians onto his side, but this work met with only mediocre results. Many of the reserves were suffering virtual starvation at the hands of tyrannical Indian Agents, so Riel's ideas found favour with some of the councils, but no solid bonds between the Métis and Indians developed during the conflict that would follow.

In the spring of 1884, Sam Steele had again transferred from the Calgary district to the CPR's constantly moving railhead in the Rocky Mountains. His headquarters was a log cabin at Beavermouth, west of Golden in British Columbia, and his task was to maintain order among the labourers or "Navvies" on the rail line. Despite being very busy everything went reasonably well until late March of 1885. The railway was experiencing cash flow problems, so the workers hadn't been paid for some time and they demanded payment. Reasonable men needed it to send part back home for family support, and the rowdies wanted to hit the bars and brothels for a long-awaited good time. As the tension grew Steele was hit by a recurrence of Rocky Mountain spotted fever, and at just the most inopportune time, he became terribly ill, bedridden.

The rail workers went on strike and a mob formed, led by some of the "hard cases." Sergeant Fury, again under Steele's command, attempted to quell the disturbance. He and the superintendent of construction warned the mob to disperse. Shortly afterward Constable Peter Kerr was sent to obtain medicine for Steele, and on his return he alone encountered the re-grouping mob. He attempted to arrest a man and received an extremely rough time, getting knocked to the ground in the hassle. Kerr retreated to the police detachment building and reported the incident. Fury responded, taking three other constables with him, and marched out to the rioters with the intent to arrest the leader. The crowd overwhelmed them and they all took a beating. Fury himself was badly pummelled, his tunic torn, and was bleeding from several cuts

Sam Steele and His Detachment—Beavermouth, B.C.
Steele is seated in the chair. Sergeant. William Fury (first on left) and
Constabe Peter Kerr (standing on far right?) would accompany
Steele as scouts on the trail of Big Bear.

before the four Mounties retreated. When Fury stumbled back to the
detachment Steele ordered the men to take their revolvers and go back,
but this time to shoot if necessary!

The intrepid men once again went back to the still growing,
belligerent crowd, seeking out the leader. Moments later a pistol shot
brought the mob to silence. A man, after attempting to interfere with
the officers who were bent on arresting another person, was gripping
his bloody shoulder. Fury had put a bullet through it!

George Johnson, the local magistrate, was with Steele when they
heard the shot. Johnson sagely commented to him, "There is one gone
to hell, Steele."

At the sound of the gunshot, Steele staggered out of his chair,
snatched a rifle from one of the constables at the door, and weakly
charged toward the retreating policemen as they dragged a prisoner back
across a wooden bridge. Sam levelled the Winchester at the enraged
mob and bellowed, "Halt! Or I shall open fire and mow you down!"

Canadian Pacific Railway Station, Calgary.
The railway changed the west forever, moving people and materials quickly and efficiently. It was also indispensable to the Alberta Field Force.

This threat brought the needed moment of silence in which Steele instructed the railway foreman to read "The Riot Act" demanding dispersal and authorizing police to fire without provocation on any assembly of more than twelve men. The threat worked; with their prisoners, Steele and his men retired to their detachment. As night fell so did a quiet peace. Within a week the pay car arrived and the tense atmosphere melded into a steady ring of sledgehammers on steel spikes again.

Sam now had a moment to reflect on a desperate message from the mayor of Calgary, imploring him to come at once for there was great fear of a general Indian uprising throughout the entire territory.

The government, in trying to force agricultural endeavours onto the Indians, refused to issue sufficient food and the treaty promises seemed as hollow as the Indians' stomachs. Conditions on the reserves were appalling. Even the government-appointed farming instructors despaired at their efforts as in 1884 there was almost a complete crop failure. Tense confrontations occurred between the NWMP and the Indians in several locales, all left to smoulder on without major bloodshed. Louis Riel continued sending out messengers to the Indians, extolling his plan. Both the Métis and the NWMP built up their forces. Colonel A. G. Irvine set out toward Prince Albert from Regina with a force of North West Mounted Police. Everything pointed towards inevitable confrontation.

At Batoche, Riel formed a provisional government in early March, and they raided several stores in the area to seize guns, ammunition, and other goods. Major Lief Crozier, in command of the North West Mounted Police at Fort Carlton, decided to remove the contents of Michell's Store at Duck Lake, halfway between Fort Carlton and Batoche, before the Métis "acquired" them. On March 26, 1885 he sent a police escorted train of sleighs to complete the task. Louis Riel and his military commander, Gabriel Dumont, led a force of Métis to intercept and forced the party to turn back to the fort. When Crozier heard of this interception he ordered 53 police and 41 Prince Albert volunteers to be loaded into sleighs, and along with a small cannon for support, set out to reinforce the first group. Unfortunately, in doing so he was unaware of Colonel Irvine's force coming from Prince Albert, which denied him of the substantial reinforcement of Prince Albert Mounties.

About three kilometres west of the town of Duck Lake, Crozier confronted the Métis force, now enlarged with Indians from a nearby reserve. An attempt at a "parlay" went sour and NWMP interpreter Joe McKay shot an Indian, Asee-wee-yin, off his horse, dead. Major Crozier then shouted a command, "Fire away boys!" The North-West Rebellion was a reality.

An intense action ensued. Crozier's force, hiding behind sleighs and lying in the snow, returned the Métis rifle fire that came from a log cabin and surrounding trees. Throughout the engagement Riel rode back and forth in full view, holding a crucifix high over his head, oblivious of the flying bullets, shouting prayers to God. The Métis' military leader Gabriel Dumont, his head grazed by a police bullet, was sprawled in the snow, semi-conscious. The police unlimbered their cannon and the untrained gunners loaded it out of sequence, rendering it useless before firing a shot. After about an hour Crozier saw his force was becoming outflanked and wisely decided to retreat. Riel noticed the police withdrawal, and in the absence of Dumont, convinced his fighters not to force themselves on the rout, averting a police surrender or annihilation. Crozier hastily retired leaving the dead: nine volunteers from Prince Albert and three Mounted Police. In contrast, the Métis had lost "only three and one Indian" (as was differentiated). Back at Fort Carlton the shattered Crozier had barely unloaded his wounded when Colonel Irvine marched his force through the gate, too late.

Word of the Duck Lake skirmish was spread amongst the Indians and Métis, as well as throughout Canada. In Ottawa, Minister of Militia Adolphe Caron ordered the pudgy, white-haired, near retirement Major General Frederick Middleton to immediately travel west to determine what was required to put down the trouble. Within days Caron received a telegram containing Middleton's evaluation of the situation and the recommendation, "Send militia, at least two-thousand." Caron initiated an immediate call up of the militia and began searching out retired officers of competence and dependability who were sprinkled throughout the territories. One such officer was Thomas Bland Strange, operator of a ranch southeast of Calgary, whom he then instructed to raise a force in the west.

On April 2, 1885, the small community of Frog Lake (north of present-day Lloydminster), became "a scene from hell" as rampaging Cree Indians, buoyed by reports of the Métis success at Duck Lake, resorted to violence to solve their own plight. The little settlement consisted of a few log houses, the Hudson's Bay store, a church, and a police detachment. Rebel warriors within Chief Big Bear's band of Cree, after being coerced by his oldest son Imassees and a War Chief Wandering Spirit, killed nine white residents, including two Roman Catholic priests and possibly several others. They chose to initiate the debacle at a church Mass just prior to Easter when all the settlers were gathered together. They forced everyone out of the little church at gunpoint, shooting and killing all the men except one, and taking captives, which included two white women of the community. They then set fire to virtually every building in the community, burning them to the ground.

More shock waves travelled throughout the country as news of this unspeakable atrocity spread. The concern over a widespread uprising had more than substantial credence. If the general Indian population joined in, the whole of the territories could be aflame with war in a matter of weeks.

A couple of weeks later the growing force of Indians surrounded Fort Pitt, a long time trading post that in 1885 was a fort only in name. During the siege NWMP Constable David Cowan was killed and Constable Clarence Loasby severely wounded.[4] Along with their guide Henry Quinn, they had attempted a desperate dash for the safety of the fort while returning from a scouting patrol to the Frog Lake settlement, and the Indians, who—understandably—mistook their rush as a charge of police cavalry, opened fire. The two Mounties were shot off their horses. The Indians were then able to pressure Inspector Francis Dickens, commander of the Fort Pitt garrison, into abandoning the indefensible trading post. In a crucial move Dickens denied the Indians armaments by destroying all the firearms and then loading his men and all the ammunition onto a leaky river scow. They silently slipped away late at night, covered by a snowstorm, and floated down the ice-choked North Saskatchewan River, eventually reaching a haven at Battleford. The civilians from the fort, taking the advice of chief trader McLean, insisted on surrendering to the Indians and as a result lived the next two months, along with the survivors of the Frog Lake murders, as prisoners in the Cree camp.

Paranoia ran rampant, but Steele could not respond without orders. Major General Thomas Bland Strange in Calgary solved the dilemma as he organized the Alberta Field Force. At the direction of Minister of Militia Adolphe Caron in Ottawa, Steele and his detachment were released to join Strange and the rebellion effort.

Thomas Bland Strange (known to all as "Gunner Jingo") was a well-respected, retired major general who trained as a gunnery officer in England, served in the East India mutinies, then travelled to Canada and was instrumental in organizing the Canadian militia. He was forced into early retirement and moved west to establish a ranch east of Calgary near Gleichen. As the tension amongst the settlers increased, he began organizing the civilian population should an uprising become a reality. He was eminently qualified to lead what he was to call the "Alberta Field Force." His orders from Ottawa were to compose a military force, march to Edmonton, then down the North Saskatchewan River to Fort Pitt. At the same time Middleton's force would march from Winnipeg to Batoche, defeat the Métis, then catch the Indians between the two forces for the final conclusion.

There was a clamour by Calgary area settlers for increased protection by the North West Mounted Police, and specifically for the renowned Inspector Sam Steele. They had heard of Steele's detachment's work in suppressing a riot and general strike by the construction workers at the CPR's railhead near Revelstoke, British Columbia. One of Strange's first functions as commander of the Alberta Field Force was to request Steele's immediate release from the railhead. He needed a dependable and aggressive cavalry and scout group as part of the Alberta Field Force, and undeniably the best man to lead that group as its commanding officer was Samuel Benfield Steele!

Chapter 2

STEELE'S SCOUTS ARE MOULDED

On April 11, 1885, the eastbound train eased to a steamy halt, the bell impatiently chiming out its presence at the newly constructed Canadian Pacific Railway station. The conductor swung down from the steps of the passenger car, dropped a wooden step stool onto the platform, then stood to the side to assist the passengers that followed. One man stood out from the others, not because of his scarlet red tunic, nor his brilliantly polished brown riding boots, or the chalk white helmet; it was his physique and carriage that drew people's attention. Samuel Benfield Steele, North West Mounted Policeman extra-ordinaire was again back in Calgary. He was the epitome of a policeman, believing fanatically in "image," and everything he did oozed it. The way he walked, sat on a horse, shot a gun, or even rested in a chair had the mark of a British military officer and the mould for a North West Mounted Policeman Steele also possessed virtually every attribute one would expect of an officer of the law in Canada: dedication, honesty, a sense of fairness, pride, courage, and supreme confidence. Everyone he encountered— white, Indian, or Métis—found him always to be a fair, genuinely respectable policeman. Steele believed in physical fitness, so his six-foot frame carried square shoulders, a burly chest, and powerful arms and legs. This man was no "stuffed shirt," but a "doer" with a reputation for endurance that had become legendary, and few men could hold pace with him in adversity. He easily outshone any great western American hero, yet here he stood, a man of far greater qualities than any of them, on a train platform in Calgary, Canada!

*Fifteen police members of Steele's Scouts (there are seventeen in photo).
This photo was probably taken in August 1885 at Battleford after
hostilities ceased. Back row, standing: Kerr, Walters, Fane, Waring,
A. Davidson, Morton, Hetherington, Whipps, Percival. Centre row,
seated: A.L. Davidson, Robinson, Dubreuil, Bunt. Front, reclining:
Richardson, McMinn, McRae, McCarthy. Fane and
A. Davidson were not officially signed on as "Scout" members.
Note: This identification has recently been discovered and has not been
previously published although the photo has been used quite often.*

Stephan (8th) Avenue, Calgary 1885.
NWMP barracks in background at end of the street.

The Calgary train station was full of men, women, children, and baggage waiting to board the train for Winnipeg and away from danger. Many residents of the town recognized him and called out a welcome back as he marched down the dirt street on his way to the Police barracks at the far, eastern end of Stephan (now 8th) Avenue. Upon entering the front door he discovered a frustrated General T. B. "Jingo" Strange sitting at a table holding a list of equipment and wondering aloud, "Why in blazes hasn't this order arrived yet? There's no reason for it not to be here—other than someone down east is just plain damn lazy!"

Strange flipped the lists onto the table and jumped up to shake hands with the policeman. He waved Steele to a chair across from him and during the next hour he explained the situation as he knew it.

"Things don't look good, Sam," he began. "Crozier had a scrap with a bunch of Métis east of Fort Carlton and took a beating, lost a dozen men. Sad thing is Irvine was only a couple hours away and could have reinforced him had he just waited a bit. They had to abandon Fort Carlton and I understand it's been burnt to the ground."

Steele listened intently as Strange continued.

"There's been a massacre of people by the Indians at Frog Lake and I have no idea how many are dead. I understand the Indians then surrounded Fort Pitt and forced Dickens to abandon it. He allowed the

Steele's Scouts are Moulded   33

Calgary, 1885.
Looking northwest, probably from "Scotchsman's Hill."

civilians of the fort to surrender—of all things! I don't know how many of them gave up, or even if they're alive now."

This news startled Steele as Fort Pitt's chief trader William J. McLean and his family were his friends. In the past he'd spent many pleasant evenings visiting in their home.

Strange continued on. "There's a lot of uneasiness amongst the local people over the situation and rumours are flying all over town about this mess spreading. Many of the settlers are moving into town, even sending their families back east on the train for the time being. I've formed a Calgary Home Guard under command of Major Walker, and Major Stewart has already organized the Rocky Mountain Rangers with Kootenai Brown in charge. In addition I've also recruited Major George Hatton to form a cowboy cavalry unit, the Alberta Mounted Rifles."[5]

Strange leaned over the table, looking Steele hard in the eye. "Steele, I need you to build a scouting force for me. I need eyes I can trust while we go after these renegades and put them in their places. Equipment is already on order but you'll have to acquire and train both your men and their horses. You are to be released from the Mounted Police and immediately appointed a major of the militia to give you proper command authority. I want to march to Edmonton as soon as possible, then down the North Saskatchewan River to meet up with General Middleton's force

Fort Pitt NWMP Detachment, 1884.
Inspector Francis Dickens, lacklustre son of novelist Charles Dickens, was in charge (bottom front right). Constable Ralph Sleigh (third row, looking at camera) and Constable David Cowan (very back row, nearest, face just visible) were both killed the next year, during the North-West Rebellion.

Fur Trading at Fort Pitt.
Big Bear, with plumed hat, is centre. Constable Ralph Sleigh (seated right, on cart) left Frog Lake at the settlers' request a day prior to the massacre, returned to Fort Pitt, endured the siege, and then floated downriver with the detachment to Fort Battleford. He was ultimately killed in the battle of Cutknife Hill on May 3, 1885.

as he comes north and west. That way we'll trap the Indians between us and put an end to this redskin uprising once and for all. Oh, in addition, I've named your contingent *Steele's Scouts*—if that's all right with you."

It was now up to Steele to build the best force he knew how. His NWMP detachment from the railhead under Sergeant Fury would arrive soon, but he would need more men than that, so he decided to enlist volunteers to bring the total strength up to about 60. Steele retained overall command, but the 25 police were under the immediate command of Lieutenant John Coryell, a graduate of Mount Royal College in Kingston, Ontario. Coryell owned land just west of town and had extensive military training despite being a land surveyor by trade. The command structure split below Steele: Coryell in charge of the police, Major Hatton in command of the 22 Alberta Mounted Rifles, and Captain James K. Oswald in charge of twenty volunteer cowboy scouts. The number of scouts would later swell beyond the original 62 during the march north and east into hostile land.

The next day, April 12, the 65th Mount Royal Rifles (the 65th) arrived on the train from Quebec dressed in their black-green uniforms and shouldering long-barrel Snyder Enfield rifles with bayonets fixed. They marched past their general, Jingo Strange, to the militia camp on the east end of Stephan Avenue—behind the police barracks—to an open area near the confluence of the Bow and Elbow Rivers. Five days later, the Winnipeg Light Infantry (WLI), bearing similar firearms but dressed in scarlet tunics and white belts, marched in a swirling spring blizzard from the train to a camp alongside the 65th regiment. The night turned for the worse and most of the tents blew down or filled with snow, forcing both regiments to cram themselves into the NWMP barracks, out of the storm.

The Alberta Field Force was growing daily despite the difficulties, but with Sergeant William Fury's help, Steele had little trouble accumulating the men he required. Some of the inductees owned property nearby: John Coryell's home was located west of the townsite of Calgary; Joseph Butlin, an ex-NWMP member, lived just south of town; and most of the other members either lived in town or worked on nearby ranches. Virtually everyone who was inducted believed this was their chance for one last great adventure and they readily put their signatures to an enlistment agreement.

Steele's Scouts Enlistment Agreement

We, the undersigned, agree to serve with the Alberta district field force for the period of six months, or so long as the present disturbance continues, in the capacity of cavalry soldiers, or mounted scouts, as may be ordered, to be subject to the militia acts and regulations.

1. To receive free blankets.

2. To receive rations and forage when the same can be procured, and in event of the same not being supplied to accept such remuneration in lieu as may be fixed by our commanding officer, or as per vouchers produced.

3. Each man to supply horse, saddlery, rifle and revolver, to be approved and passed by our commanding officer. Should the same be supplied by the commanding officer the articles supplied are to be his property until paid for by deductions from pay, which he is authorized to make under the agreement.

4. Rifle and revolver, supplied by Government, to be taken back in good condition.

5. Men to be classed for pay as follows:
    1st class per day $2.50
    2nd class per day $2.25
    3rd class per day $2.00

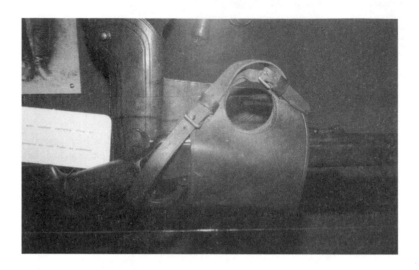

Leather Thong Rifle Holster with Issue 45–75 Winchester.
The Winchester is a lever action rifle. The saddle horn went through the hold and the rifle hung crossways to the rider in front of the saddle.

The *Calgary Bulletin* newspaper editorially calculated the pay as $2.50 per day, totalling $225.00. Costs for a horse were estimated at $150.00, a saddle at $50.00, and incidentals at $10.00 to equal a total of $210.00. At the end of his service with the force, the article claimed, a scout would have $15.00 in his pocket!

Steele chose his equipment wisely. Strange had seen to the choice of headgear already, wisely choosing very broad-brimmed cowboy hats with the left side jauntily pinned up. These were issued to everyone in his force—scouts, cavalry, and infantry—as a protective requirement from the elements. They gave shade from burning sun, kept rain from running down the neck, and the brims could be tied down over the ears when it was cold. During a discussion with Sam, Jingo jokingly suggested the police might reverse their conspicuous red tunics, putting the dull-coloured lining on the outside, but Sam, perceiving the jovial mood, testily replied, "Sir, my men are not turncoats!" They both broke into laughter, but the point was made. By refusing to give up the red tunic Steele was the only one of his scouts to wear the traditional police dress during the campaign. The police scouts deferred the red tunics for their brown canvas stable jackets but retained the dark blue, yellow-striped pants. In this way they still maintained a separate identity from the rest of the scouts.[6] Strange himself chose an old pair of blue police riding breeches that had a gold stripe down the side, a buckskin jacket, and the issue cowboy hat with three gold braids around the brim, signifying his rank. As formal dress he wore a dark blue frock coat with epaulets on the shoulders. On his belt he hitched his old militia sword, taken off the ranch house wall.

Nothing in the scouts' equipment was to jingle or clatter, so leather, rope, and even wooden stirrups were chosen with this in mind. The police retained the issued Adams .450 calibre revolver, and everyone other than Steele was issued superb new eight-shot Winchester lever action, 45-75 calibre rifles to replace the antiquated single shot Snyder-Enfield carbine issue. Many of the volunteers supplied their own revolvers and ammunition. Steele's Scouts were initially allotted 300 rounds of ammunition each for their rifles, indicating the expectation of serious encounters before the campaign closed.

Their trail kit contained a change of underclothes, rolled and tied behind the saddle, and a slicker rolled in front, beside which hung a lariat that doubled as a picket rope. The rifle was carried crosswise in front of the saddle by using a wide leather strap. It was attached to the saddle horn and fashioned so that it could be unhooked quickly when the rider wanted to use it. This method of carrying the rifle was preferred—over putting the rifle in a scabbard or "bucket"—by all of the mounted scouts. Ammunition was carried in bandoliers slung over the shoulder or around the waist with a reserve supply in the saddlebags.

They trained the horses to remain steady when the rider was shooting by firing off a pistol at each feeding time. Most of the half-wild cayuses (common term for prairie ponies) acquired for the scouts were not even broken to ride. The resulting rodeo provided an alternative entertainment to card games for the militia soldiers during the days prior to marching. Much of the training of both horses and men had to continue as the column advanced northward since Strange could not delay any more than necessary.

Most of the other commanders under Strange were faced with a similar problem. Steele occasionally had a moment to watch as the militia recruits attempted to become proficient with the cumbersome Snyder-Enfield and Martini-Henry rifles. These old muzzle-loading firearms had been converted to fire large .58-calibre cartridges, made by soldering a couple of wraps of thin brass sheet to a moulded brass base, which held the primer. The heavy bullet, propelled with black powder, had a low muzzle velocity and was not particularly accurate at long range. Military testing records of the two brands of rifles indicate the Martini-Henry rifle to be the more accurate of the two. Many of the young soldiers had rarely fired a rifle before and even Indian witnesses to their training took delight in remarking on their atrocious marksmanship. Many were unable to hit a metre square target at only 175 metres of range. On the other hand, the Indians were astonished by the ritual-like precision of bayonet drill that the militiamen conducted.

The cowboys and scouts dressed in direct contrast to the militia's sharp looking uniforms. They wore buckskin jackets, large leather schappes (protective leggings), revolvers, Bowie knives, and bandoliers of ammunition. They drew undivided attention; soldiers wrote letters back home describing their wild habits, riding half drunk at a full gallop, shooting at and hitting their targets with seeming ease. The scene was indelibly printed in the minds of most of the easterners as truly being the "wild west." These same letters also contained complaints about the price gouging by local merchants for eggs, milk, sweets, and extra clothing. Some examples indicated the prices charged in 1885 were comparable or in excess of what we pay today in a supermarket.

John A. Coryell accepted a lieutenant's position, under Sam Steele. On April 15 Coryell was ordered to march on the Red Deer crossing, to cross the river, and attempt to occupy it until the arrival of the main force. His small group of fifteen scouts were to support the local settlers in establishing a defensible position using whatever means available. Should they be attacked they were to fall back to Strange's main force, which would be marching towards them. Coryell's force had little difficulty carrying out the orders other than several members suffering temporary snow blindness from the sunny, springtime glare off the surrounding countryside. General Middleton's force, coming from the east, had been issued with goggles to prevent this temporary malady but none were available to the scout group. The embarrassing affliction was severe enough in Coryell's case that he had to be led by one of his scouts until his eyes recovered a couple of days later.

About the same time the renowned Reverend John McDougall was dispatched with four Stony Indian scouts to traverse the route to

Edmonton, evaluating the state of the Indians along the way, and notifying residents the Field Force was on the march and expected to arrive in a few days. He was able to accomplish the task and scout-courier the valuable information back to Strange.

On April 20 Strange was ready to march. The column consisted of over 400 men, 175 transport wagons lead by General Strange, and his personal wagon driven by Wheeler Mickle. Mickle's wagon had a long buggy whip attached to the front seat and pinned to that was a "sixpenny cotton pocket handkerchief with the Union Jack painted on it," the only battle flag of the Alberta Field Force.

The Alberta Field Force camp was located on the east end of 8th Avenue where Fort Calgary Historical Park is now located. Reference to old maps shows many of the prominent members of the force lived nearby: Coryell on the south side of the Shaganappi Golf Course, Joseph Butlin in the Glenmore Athletic Park area, and Colonel Walker to the east of Butlin's. Calgary's main street was then named Stephan Avenue, later to be re-named 8th Avenue.

In 1885, military competence was still a dominating factor in the choice of commanding officers. All had military training from the Royal Military College at Kingston, or from old England. The choices of leadership were made with a view to warfare and not a "policing action," and for this reason, Coryell was commanding the police contingent of the scouts despite not being a policeman, and Steele was the chief commanding officer of the three. Records of Steele and Strange clearly show a marked "Imperial" preferential status: Military, Police, English origin, Cowboy, Métis, then Indian. The exception is Strange's affection for the French 65th Mount Royal Rifles whom he regarded very highly because of his past association with them down east while he was still a serving officer.

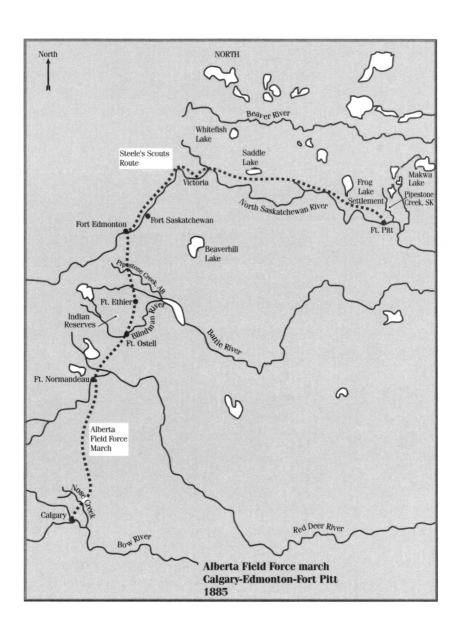

**Alberta Field Force march
Calgary-Edmonton-Fort Pitt
1885**

Chapter 3

THE MARCH TO EDMONTON

On April 19, 1885 General Strange held a briefing with his commanders at his Calgary headquarters—the NWMP barracks. Those that attended included: Captain C.H. Dale, Brigade Major; Major Steele, Steele's Scouts; Colonel George Hughes, 65th Mount Royal Rifles; Colonel William Osborne-Smith, Winnipeg Light Infantry; Major George Hatton, Alberta Mounted Rifles Cavalry; Captain Wright, Transport and Supply; and Harry Strange (Jingo's son), Aide-de-camp. Strange began the meeting by saying, "Gentlemen, we're all aware of the situation to the northeast. General Middleton is preparing to march his force to attack the Métis at their heart, Batoche. Colonel Otter is marching from Fort Qu' Appelle north to Battleford, where there is unrest on the nearby reserves, and it is our duty to march from here to Edmonton, then downstream along the North Saskatchewan River to Fort Pitt where we will establish a base of operations. Middleton's force and ours will work toward each other, catching the rebels in the middle. In this way we expect to quash this uprising, once and for all. Colonel Otter is to remain at Battleford to keep an eye on the Indians there and—if need be—to act as reinforcement should it be required. Colonel Irvine is at Prince Albert with the same instructions. Now to business: First off, out of necessity I must split the force temporarily into three columns. I will take the first column with me in the morning. It consists of Captain Dale, Brigade Major, who is my second in command, and Major Steele and his scouts, who will act as the eyes for our column and also provide a warning against attacks. Colonel Hughes and half of his Mount Royal Rifles (Voltigeurs) will also march with us in the morning, and Captain Wright will accompany this first column with half the supplies.

"The second column must wait for their equipment to arrive but will march as soon as they possibly can. That group includes Captain and Inspector Bowen Perry of the North West Mounted Police. They are coming from Fort Macleod along with the field-gun, and the second half of the Voltigeurs as well as a medical officer and outfit. I expect them to catch up to us at Edmonton. The last column, with Osborne-Smith in charge, will include his Light Infantry, Hatton's Alberta Mounted Rifles, and Captain Hamilton with the additional supply wagons, along with Chief Medical Officer Surgeon-Major Pennefather and his medical wagons. Because of their late departure, this last column will have to cut across

General Thomas Bland Strange.
Commander of the Alberta Field Force, Strange was a noticeable character because of his exaggerated erect posture.

country toward Fort Pitt and intercept us on the trail. It's not the best plan, but it must do since speed in showing a military response to the Indian rebels is of upmost importance in returning stability to the territory again. Daily orders will be posted on Mickle's wagon, which will be beside my tent. I hope to commence the march north tomorrow in mid-afternoon."

Fort Edmonton 1885.
Fort was located where present Legislative Buildings now stand.
Trail leading up the riverbank is approximately where High Level
bridge is located today. This sketch made by Captain Rutherford,
using an early photograph he borrowed as reference.

The route chosen by Strange for the first and second columns was simply to follow the existing stagecoach trail to Edmonton. Strange also warned the commanders of what he expected to encounter as the force-marched northward. For example, the Indians had burnt off the surrounding countryside north of Calgary, so there would be no firewood or grass for the horses. Whatever feed and firewood the force required had to be transported with them on the wagons.

General Middleton's unique edict was for the absence of alcohol in all the forces involved in the rebellion. Most military forces of the day relied on a regular issue of rum for each man to "ward off the chill"; however, in this campaign neither Middleton nor Strange provided for such a luxury. Some individuals did sneak along their own small supply but as a general rule it was a "dry" campaign. Strange also did not allow any game hunting, prudently fearing the shooting would be confused with an attack, or worse, an attack would be initially ignored by the soldiers, thinking it was someone shooting at a rabbit or grouse.

Strange's second column included Inspector A. Bowen Perry's twenty NWMP, their nine-pound cannon, and 150 rounds of ammunition in its caisson. They had marched out of Fort Macleod and would pick up four companies of the 65th Mount Royal Rifles at Calgary on April 23. Then they would catch up to Strange in Edmonton while he was there preparing defences prior to moving eastward. The third column, with Colonel Osborne Smith leading the remaining companies of the Winnipeg Light Infantry, Major Hatton's Alberta Mounted Rifles, and the surgeon Pennefather's medical wagons, would start out even later on April 28, endeavouring to catch up by cutting across country on a trail that approximately parallelled the Battle River. The new saddles for the Mounted Rifles were deplorable; most of them were of such poor quality they had to be rebuilt to prevent immediate failure. This last group was leaving Calgary late due to the time required for saddle repair and the slow delivery of additional equipment from the east. All three columns would not fully re-unite again until May 23, at Dog Rump Creek, near Elk Point.

During the morning of April 20, the column struck camp and spent most of the day forming up. General Strange, astride his big chestnut horse, dressed in a buckskin jacket, broad-brimmed hat with its left side pinned up, and a sword on his belt gave a short bilingual speech to the militia troops. He complimented them on their spirit and warned of adversity to come, speaking a portion in good French—to the amazement and pleasure of the 65th Voltigeurs (the 65th) from Montreal—as he described their past heritage and their reputation for loyalty to their regiment in always getting the job done. When Strange finally gave the order to march at about four in the afternoon, a fife and drum corps from the Winnipeg regiment played them through Calgary to the river ford at the edge of town.

Some of the scouts' partially trained cayuses began to buck at the sound of the band and a frenzied rodeo ensued as the riders tried to settle them down again. Sadly shaking his head, Jingo's rueful opinion about the pandemonium was its worthiness of inclusion in Buffalo Bill's Wild West Show! The column marched to the Bow River ford at the Eau Claire sawmill site, across the river, up the North Hill, and then northward on the Edmonton trail.

Steele, in his habitually immaculate red tunic, pipe clay-coloured gauntlet gloves, and out of character "cowboy hat" led the column with his scouts. Other scouts were assigned to ride on each flank and a final group acted as a rear guard of the column. Once they reached open country the scouts spread out, Steele leading some about a kilometre ahead with other "flankers" a similar distance to each side. By positioning them in this fashion Steele provided not only eyes for General Strange but also a warning should the column come under attack by hostile Indians.

The column followed the Edmonton trail northward from the Bow River to a ford of Nose Creek. The stream was running swiftly with high water from the melting snow, so this crossing proved an insight into future creek crossings. The stream bank turned soft and became grease slippery and many of the horses pulling the wagons experienced difficulty hauling them through. In due time the troops learned to attach ropes to the wagons and augment the horses with ten or twenty men heaving on the lines as the wagons came up the bank.

Just north of the Nose Creek crossing Steele chose a bivouac for the column's first night; the wagons were formed into a circle, and 40 men were detailed to sentry duty, posted about one and a half kilometres from camp and about two hundred metres apart. Outside the perimeter of sentries, Steele's Scouts circulated on horseback, occasionally extending out 30 kilometres or more, checking creek banks, trails, and hilltops for unshod pony tracks or signs of recent Indian camps. They were to provide flawless security for the force the entire distance to Edmonton.

The tents were pitched, and supper was cooked outside the circle of wagons and supplies. This allowed the armed soldiers to protect them if hostiles should attack with the intent of setting them afire. Strange discovered his cook was capable of miracles with pork fat, canned meat, and flour, deserving a medal for his efforts. Strange intimated he should have been awarded the coveted military medal, the D.S.C. (Damn Smart Cook)! The other militia's and scouts' meals varied with the state of the supplies but were not like our modern, well-balanced meals as vegetables were usually considered a luxury for them. The fare was simple, being usually beef or pork, beans or potatoes, biscuits, and tea.

The first day had been traditionally a "Hudson's Bay start"—a short march of about only ten kilometres to their first bivouac. This was a common practice of the day, allowing the column members an opportunity to easily retrieve last-minute forgotten items from their base.

At 4:30 a.m. the trumpeter's bugle notes of "Reveille" for the Alberta Field Force accompanied the first faint streaks of dawn in the eastern sky. The "tents down" command came at 5:10, followed by "Advance" being sounded exactly an hour later. Rest halts were called every hour and a half, giving the militia an opportunity to tend sore feet and to practise judging distance by sighting their empty rifles on the mounted scouts patrolling adjacent to the column. At times Strange found the column's advance frustratingly slow and extended, stretching two and three kilometres in length. He solved this by ordering the wagons, where practical, to travel six abreast. The column averaged about 29 kilometres each day—a distance considered quite a respectable rate of march for a militia force even under ideal conditions. The second day brought on some really bad weather as a spring blizzard hit the column with wet snow that stuck to the soldiers' coats like a coat of white paint. Despite the blowing swirling storm the march continued all day until Steele finally chose McPherson's Coulee as an overnight stop and camp was set up.

On the next morning, April 22, ignoring the lingering snowstorm, camp routine was followed as it normally would despite everything being frozen solid. "Tent pegs had to be chopped out of the ground by the men, the ropes were like steel rods, the tents themselves could only be folded and heaped on the wagons," Jingo recorded in his journal. "The storm blew all day making the march cold, wet and miserable for the men so at noon a 40-minute halt was called for a lunch of bullybeef and hardtack biscuits." These biscuits—a combination of flour, baking powder, and water—were the mainstay of the force on the march. They rarely spoiled, just simply got harder, and the soldiers joked they would make excellent cannon ammunition if the "gun team" began to run low. The tinned meat was an early version of military rations: chopped beef cooked and sealed in the can with lead solder (lead contamination was unknown in 1885). The style of can was similar to a modern rectangular can of hot chocolate mix with the round lid on the top. A soldier simply threw it on a fire to heat, and when the round lid's solder melted and fell off, the contents were ready to eat. The can was hacked open with a knife, which also became the eating utensil.

Steele's Scouts had their work cut out for them that morning probing around and finally locating the faint trail under fifteen centimetres of snow in a complete "white-out." Typical of this part of the country, in the afternoon a clear blue chinook arch spread across the western sky and a warm wind began to blow, quickly melting the white blanket away. That night the column camped a few kilometres north of Scarlett's roadhouse, a stagecoach stopping place.

To speed the column's march, Strange decided to order an advance party ahead of them to prepare the soft spots with corduroy, slope the creek crossings, and clear trees. An ex-NWMP, Sergeant George Borradaile, volunteered to lead the group, taking six lumberjack axemen from the 65th, three scouts, and two days' supplies. They started out at 4:00 a.m. on this potentially dangerous task despite other scouts reporting signs of Indians monitoring the march's progress. Occasionally they would see mirror flashes from warriors signalling back and forth, or the distant puffs of smoke signal fires. Borradaile's "pioneer crew" of trail builders succeeded in staying ahead of the column despite the danger. His three guard-scouts patrolled a perimeter, keeping watch while the construction crew concentrated on their work of improving the trail.

April 23 finally brought the column to the first sparse trees that interrupted the blackened, barren prairie of the past two days' travel. They made their way around some of the bluffs occasionally deviating from the existing stagecoach trail as it progressed northward. The weather continued to improve and the snow melted quickly during the sunny warm spring days. Despite the incessant marching, it became a more pleasant task for the militia, treading along, listening to the crows, and seeing the first tips of green grass and blooming crocuses on the hillsides.

Steele marvelled at the scenery as he rode. If the mission was not so foreboding it might well have been a holiday outing. During the column's rest breaks the recruit soldiers practised and learned the techniques of their new trade. Many of them were just out of school, not more than twenty, some having never fired a rifle; and only a few of the junior officers could rely on any past combat experience whatsoever. Often it was Jingo Strange, who drew on his India soldiering, or Steele or Sergeant Fury recalling early militia experience that provided the training that made the militiamen's lives more tolerable. They instructed the men in battle techniques such as placing three cartridges pointing downward between the fingers of the left hand while holding the rifle up to fire. This trick allowed them to reload the single shot rifles relatively quickly without having to fumble in their pouches for another round each time.

This night the force camped about ten kilometres south of the Lone Pine—a distinct stand of trees with one giant single pine amongst them. There was also a stopping house nearby for travellers from Edmonton to Calgary.

The fourth day of the march found the Field Force settled down to a routine. The scout horses weren't causing quite so much trouble, the men had camp set-up and take-down refined, but the food began to get monotonous. That morning the cooks of the 65th negligently left their fires burning when they began the day's march. When this inexcusable sin of abandoning a potential source of a prairie fire was discovered, the diligent rear guard scouts put out the fires and reported the incident. Strange disciplined the delinquent cooks by ordering them to march all day, on foot, under escort. The incident was not to be repeated again during the campaign.

Toward the end of each day some of the militia were able to ride on the wagons, especially the sentries and scouts of the night before, so they dozed as the wagons clattered on. As the provisions were used up more wagons became free for troop transport. When the column drew closer to the Indian reserves and the threat of attack increased, Strange ordered the sentries to now conduct their watches with loaded guns. For the night of April 24, Steele selected a bivouac at the confluence of two creeks known as "The Forks."

Unknown to Strange, General Middleton was engaged in a battle with Métis forces at Fish Creek, south of Batoche. His militia had approached a ravine south of the village, where the Métis were lying in wait for him at a trail crossing of the creek. The battle was initially fierce with some of the Métis riflemen making good use of their buffalo rifles to pick off the cannon's gun teams whenever they reloaded. As the troops exchanged fire with the Métis forces Captain James Peters used the opportunity to take the first combat photographs in the history of Canada. The battle eventually dwindled to sporadic shooting as evening approached, and Middleton's corps settled into a defensive

Militia Firing Line, Battle of Fish Creek.
*This photo, one of the first combat photos in Canadian history, was
taken by Captain James Peters at Fish Creek. The Métis' forces are
just over the rise in the valley to the right.*

position for the night. The Métis force vanished with the twilight, falling
back to the settlement of Batoche.

April 25 brought the Alberta Field Force to the crossing at the Red
Deer River. Borradaile's group had done some preliminary work, but
there was still no ferry operating due to the recent break-up of the river
ice. All of the wagons were modified to keep the equipment and supplies
drier, by using blocks of wood to raise the boxes higher over the axles.
The north bank of the river was an ideal location for an ambush, covered
with dense willow, poplar, and alder, reducing visibility to nearly
nothing. It was so dense it prevented the scouts from crossing and
dispersing on horseback, so Jingo Strange personally lead the 65th across,
riding on the wagons with their rifles loaded and ready. On the far
shore the soldiers jumped out and quickly extended in skirmish order,
probing the bush for the expected hostiles. No resistance was
encountered at the river even though Indian smoke signals in the distance
continued to warn of their presence at the ford. The wagon-borne force
returned to their camp on the south side later in the day, leaving the
scouts to occupy and patrol the north side of the river.

That night the column camped on the south side of the river. Strange ordered Lieutenant J. Bedard Normandeau and twenty men of the 65th to remain at the crossing to construct a fort to act as a defence base, protecting the Edmonton to Calgary supply line. It took this contingent about six weeks to construct buildings of squared logs inside a stockade, erected by placing trees vertically into a trench. Three bastions were built into the wall, providing a field of fire along the face of the stockade. A moat was also constructed around the outside to further enhance the fortification. The fort commander was allowed to name Fort Normandeau in honour of himself, thus insuring an excellent job would be done.

In addition to Fort Normandeau, the 65th Mount Royal Rifles built two other forts during their stay in Alberta. The second was Fort Ostell, which consisted of a new bastion added to the existing Hudson's Bay Company post. Because of the proximity of the Indian reserves Captain John Ostell's company was understandably nervous. As part of the fortification, trenches two metres deep were dug around its perimeter. One settler wryly claimed that whenever enthusiasm waned it only took the appearance of one Indian to instantly rejuvenate the soldiers' incentive. He declared that the fortifications they created could have repelled even Napoleon's army.

The third fort was Fort Ethier constructed in the Peace Hills under the direction of Captain L. J. Ethier. It was of similar construction to the others, but being in even closer proximity to the reserve, was more threatened. Ethier claimed in a letter written on May 5 that on several occasions his sentries had been shot at and the fort frequently attacked—albeit ineptly— by Indians at night. None of the forts were required to repulse a concerted attack by the foe that most certainly originated from Ermineskin's and Bobtail's reserves. The forts served their purpose in maintaining safe transport of supplies from Calgary to Edmonton, aiding significantly in keeping the peace and preventing a serious spread of hostilities.

April 26 was occupied at the Red Deer River. Strange ordered a complete reorganization of the column's supplies. There was no longer a need to carry wood, feed for the horses, or for all the provisions they had brought. Everything was sorted and the unnecessary supplies sent back to Calgary along with any empty wagons. At the same time, Steele had Lieutenant Coryell, who had in the meantime recovered from his snow blindness condition, take ten scouts and two companies of the 65th Voltigeurs across the river and establish another bivouac there. By afternoon the rest of the column had followed, so the rest of the day was again used for training and practise.

The next day, April 27, Strange wanted to increase the pace, so the militia was divided into three shifts—two marching and one riding on the wagons. The terrain became extremely boggy, and the soldiers tired from the constant exertion of trudging through over-the-ankle-deep spring mud already churned up by the lead units of the column. Some deviously attempted to lighten the load by slipping their rifles into the wagons, resulting in the officers keeping a keen eye to prevent it. A soldier was of little value without his rifle.

The Field Force marched to the Blindman River crossing located in a deep ravine—another location ideally suited to an ambush. Borradaile's brave pioneer group, despite their vulnerability of being trapped in the

Sergeant George Borradaile
A retired NWMP in charge of General Strange's "Pioneer Scouts" preceded the Alberta Field Force, preparing the trail. He also volunteered to be a messenger between Strange and Middleton, canoeing down the North Saskatchewan River, through dangerous, hostile country to Fort Battleford.

Canon George McKay
*McKay (shortest, centre, middle row and inset),
also called the "fighting preacher," packed his
bible—along with his ammunition—in his saddle
bags. Fluent in Cree, he was indispensable to Steele as
a scout, taking on many of the most dangerous tasks.*

gorge by a hostile force, had completely repaired the partially burned bridge, making it again serviceable. This location was by far the most dangerous position the pioneer construction crew faced. In a matter of minutes Indian warriors on attack could have easily wiped them out.

That evening at the Blindman River crossing, a preacher, Reverend George McKay, rode into camp. After 320 kilometres of hard riding all the way from Fort Macleod, bypassing Calgary, he had finally caught up to the column. The self-proclaimed "Fighting Preacher," a canon of the Anglican Church, spoke Cree fluently and was widely known for handling a Winchester or Colt just as well as his Bible.

As his dark piercing eyes flashed, he explained to an amused Sam, "My Bible and prayer book rode along in the saddlebag—here with my extra cartridges!" He was a welcome addition to Steele's Scouts; although being shown on the records as their chaplain, this "gun fighting preacher" helped both Steele and Strange in particularly risky scouting tasks throughout the campaign against Big Bear.

April 29 provided the entire column with their first exposure to Indians since the start of the march. While they were camped at the Battle River, Steele intercepted Father Albert Lacombe and Father Constantine Scollen who were accompanied by two chiefs, Ermineskin and Bobtail, from the nearby reserves. They intended to meet the general, implying peaceful co-operation with the Queen's force. Steele was not a bit impressed with the two natives, calling them the worst of the "coffeecoolers" with a prior reputation for listless languishing around the trading posts. Father Scollen complimented Ermineskin and Bobtail as he had little use for "the British," being a sympathizer of Fenian rebel beliefs. Steele was sceptical of all but Father Lacombe whom he suspected was likely responsible for maintaining relative calm in the district

General Strange held back and would not meet with them, even refusing the Indian custom of shaking hands, deferring that ritual for when he would return—provided they behaved themselves. Instead Jingo formed up his column and "quick marched" his men through their reserves in a show of force. Initially, the Indians who peered through the bush or stood alongside the trail were not impressed by the dark green uniforms of the 65th Voltigeurs, but the scarlet outfits of the Winnipeg Light Infantry who followed afterwards was another matter. The red tunics of this force with a display of "fixed bayonets" on their rifles convinced them the force of the white Queen was present and not to be trifled with.

Steele's suspicions were proven correct when a family of settlers along with the Hudson's Bay store manager came into camp on their way to the protection of Fort Normandeau, complaining bitterly of their buildings been pillaged just days earlier by these same Indians.

The column reached Pipestone Creek the afternoon of the next day. Strange received a message by a hard riding scout courier from Inspector Griesbach at Fort Saskatchewan requesting support. He and his force of ten policemen was host to a growing group of settlers seeking safety. Despite clearing about three hundred metres of brush and building a bastion, he felt the fort was vulnerable and not defensible from a concerted attack; he requested that Strange supply additional militia defensive support. Strange responded to the request the next day when his column was near Edmonton.

On May 1, 1885 Strange formed up his column for the last leg of the Calgary to Edmonton journey. As they marched toward the old fort, grateful settlers drove out to meet them, offering transport for the troops in their wagons as well as expressing gratitude and relief. Strange graciously declined the offers, recognizing the boost of pride his force would feel in marching smartly into Edmonton. Strange lead the force, Mickle was in the first wagon with the Union Jack flying from the buggy whip, and the sunburned militia marched in their columns, rifles proudly resting easily on their shoulders. Steele's Scouts still retained their flanking positions, but in close formation.

Across the North Saskatchewan, the town above old Fort Edmonton was wild with the excitement of the force's arrival. From the top of the fort's flagstaff a Hudson's Bay Company ensign fluttered in the breeze. The flag was a composite of the Union Jack in the top corner on a field of red and the large white "H B C" letters in the bottom opposite corner. One of the young cowboy scouts, seeing the "H B C" for the first time, wondered aloud to his partner as they rode closer, "What's the 'H B C' mean?" His buckskin clad, older partner retorted, "Here Before Christ, I guess!"

The fort's gunners, who were part of the Edmonton Home Guard, were prepared. The fire equipment, small armament, and cannon were already concentrated inside the old fort under guard. The gun team quickly loaded the pathetically small and antiquated brass cannon, preparing a welcome salute; but in their enthusiasm the ramrod ended up being left in the barrel. John Collins, the gunner, not noticing this "little detail" set off the charge. With a resounding "boom" the ramrod shot out the barrel and arched across the river, never to be found again!

Strange describes his memory of Edmonton as they approached: "The scattered little town of Edmonton, peeping through clumps of Pine and Poplar, the blue sky and brilliant sunshine gilding the grey old stockades of the Hudson's Bay Fort with it's quaint bastions and buildings crowning the steep bank over the broad, swift sweep of the Saskatchewan."

The column used John Walters' ferry to cross the river and then smartly marched up the hill past the fort and townsite to bivouac just north of today's downtown Eaton's Centre. One company of the 65th was detailed to continue to march as promised, downstream to Fort Saskatchewan, about 32 kilometres away. Once there, they were garrisoned, providing relief to that small community and the undermanned, defending detachment of police under Inspector Griesbach.

General Strange asserted of Steele's Scouts: "That the Force reached its destination in safety was, I believe, due to the precautions taken, but especially to the careful scouting of Major Steele's Force."

A fitting tribute for a job well done!

Fort Normandeau Today
The modern reproduction of Fort Normandeau,
just west of Highway #2 near Red Deer, Alberta.

Red Deer River Ford
This ford is located at Fort Normandeau. The river was in full flood when
the Alberta Field Force reached it in 1885. Hostile natives were expected
to be waiting to spring a trap in the dense bush on the far side.

General Strange recorded the Alberta Field Force covered an average of about 29 kilometres each day on its march to Edmonton. The march route followed the stagecoach trail that over the years developed into Highway #2A. After crossing the Bow River in Eau Claire they moved up the North Hill, along the Edmonton trail; then they crossed Nose Creek just west of the International Airport on April 20. The next day, April 21, the force marched along the east side of the creek, northward to where they bivouacked at McPherson's Coulee, which is about six kilometres north of Airdrie. This location is easily recognizable from the four-lane highway. On April 22 their camp was established near a roadhouse on the stage trail known as Scarlett, which was near Carstairs. They progressed on April 23 to about ten kilometres south of Olds at Lone Pine. The next day, April 24, they reached a confluence of two creeks in the Innisfail area known as "The Forks."

The crossing of the Red Deer River was accomplished on the morning of April 26 at Fort Normandeau, west of the city of Red Deer. This fort, built while the main force continued marching east, is located just west of Highway #2. It is a well-marked major tourist attraction with reconstructed buildings and interpretive centre, open to visitors from May 1 to October 15 each year. Unlike 1885, the Red Deer River appears sedate today because of a control structure upstream at the Dixon dam that has a calming effect on the passing current. April 27 saw the force on the south side of the Blindman River near Blackfalds, and the next day moved to just north of Lacombe. On the April 29 they reached the Battle River, just south of Ponoka. By April 30 Strange had the column as far as the Pipestone Creek, near Millet. The last day of the march to Edmonton was May 1, when they crossed the river on the ferry to conclude the last leg of the northward journey.

Chapter 4

DOWN THE NORTH SASKATCHEWAN

As Sam Steele and his scouts rode off the ferry and up the hill past the old fort, the town of Edmonton's relieved population clapped and cheered them in. Looking amongst the throng, he spotted his brother James grinning up at him, as he rode past to where the force established the force's bivouac at the race track on the north side of town. James had settled east of Edmonton near Beaver Lake, and in the summer he taught school for the other homesteaders nearby. Sam hadn't seen him for quite some time although they corresponded regularly as did the other members of the Steele family. The two were able to get together over the next few days, and once while James was having tea with Sam and Captain Oswald he attempted to convince them that he should accompany the force east. Despite James' desire it was apparent he'd have to remain behind, tending the farm, and upholding his teaching responsibility when school opened up. James lamented in his diary entry of May 12, 1885: "I'm hauling rails when I should be with the men."

Sam suggested to Strange that he needed additional scouts since his existing group had clearly been taxed on the march from Calgary to Edmonton. Strange agreed, admitting it was only good fortune that no serious incidents had occurred. He further ordered Steele to recruit some of the disbanded Edmonton Home Guard as well. The men Steele chose were all familiar with the country to the east and some were fluent in the Cree language. Like the Calgary inductees, the Edmonton volunteers possessed special skills or were retired militia and police members. Men such as William Stiff and Arthur Patton (who were farming on the south side of the river in the present-day university area), William

Fort Edmonton Interior, 1884.
The days of protective fortifications were virtually over by this time.
Thriving communities sprang up nearby as settlers
moved into western Canada after the transcontinental railway was built.

Ibbotson, the Roland brothers, and Métis such as John Whitford would prove to be great assets to the scouts. In addition, William Parker, a sergeant, and Joseph Chabot, a trumpeter of the NWMP posted at Fort Saskatchewan, managed to acquired leave from Inspector Griesbach, and joined the police section of the scouts.

The paranoia in Fort Edmonton and the surrounding district over the revolt caused virtual chaos in the community. Guards manning the old fort's bastions heard unnerving noises, saw shadows, and had themselves believing every clump of bush had Indians lurking behind it. False rumours abounded; it was said Victoria had been attacked, even Fort Saskatchewan had been attacked, and Indians were within a few kilometres that very moment on their way to attack Fort Edmonton. One scare turned out to be a flock of honking Canada geese flying over town; Inspector Griesbach's prowling house cat, which someone mistook for a stalking hostile, caused another!

Captain Constantine of the Winnipeg Light Infantry by chance encountered a half-breed from the Laboucane settlement and immediately arrested him after he found a letter on the man, which was originally written by a Métis at Batoche. It detailed a recent battle at

Fish Creek between themselves and General Middleton's militia. The letter's author claimed the daylong fight had been like shooting buffalo, and they had achieved a resounding victory over the militia.

Jingo Strange read the letter with some scepticism but decided to forward it on to Middleton with the other communications for his information if nothing else. Shortly after intercepting this letter, a message arrived from the general confirming the events related in the letter. "We have lost six men and almost 50 wounded at Fish Creek." The rebellion suppression was not going particularly well, and a third defeat appeared to be in the making west of Battleford.

Colonel William Otter had marched a column of troops from Swift Current to Battleford on General Middleton's orders. When he arrived at the old fort and settlement he learned Chief Poundmaker was camped about 65 kilometres west and the belief was that he was preparing to attack the fort. The Indians of the whole region had been acting belligerently for some time and Otter intended to punish them for their actions by making a pre-emptive strike. He took 325 men, two small cannons, and a Gatling gun (a predecessor of the machine gun) and marched out of the fort on the night of May 1 for Cutknife Hill.

On a high plateau just north of Cutknife Hill he located a large Cree village and commenced the attack just after dawn on May 2. The ensuing battle lasted all morning, but the Indians stopped his force in its tracks. The Cree were initially fearful of being overwhelmed but soon realized their defensive advantage. Otter's lightweight cannon fire proved to be just a noisy irritation as the warriors fired from the trees, picking off soldiers and police, one by one. The antiquated old field guns' rotted wooden mounts fell apart after firing only a few rounds, rendering both of them useless. Wisely, Otter recognized his predicament and was able to withdraw under the covering fire of the remaining Gatling gun, sustaining eight dead and fourteen wounded.[7] He must have felt fortunate indeed that he had not been overrun as General Custer had in the battle of The Little Big Horn.

Poundmaker's losses were only five dead and three wounded. He was later to proclaim:

> "It would be so much easier just to fold our hands and
> not make this fight. To say I, one man can do nothing.

Mounted Police Defensive Training.
Both horses and men were trained in using this emergency defensive position. This demonstration was photographed in the early 1900s.

I grow afraid only when I see people thinking and acting like this. We all know the story about the man who sat beside the trail too long, and then it grew over and he could never find his way again. We can never forget what has happened, but we cannot go back nor can we sit beside the trail!"[8]

This statement is indicative of Poundmaker's belief the government had forced him into a fight and he was not prepared to stand by and do nothing. It was only through good fortune for the Canadian government that a subsequent union with Big Bear's warriors did not occur. Had Poundmaker's and Big Bear's men joined together the unrest in the territories may well have erupted into a bloody war within the triangle of Fort Pitt, Battleford, and Batoche, creating a major crisis that Ottawa may not have controlled.

While the Field Force was waiting for the last two columns to arrive from Calgary, additional preparation work and training continued. The scout horses were still not completely comfortable with gunfire, especially when their riders shot from their backs, so some of the training was conducted next to the militia's firing range. The civilian scouts had to be instructed on military jargon, bugle calls, and procedures; others required rifle practice with the unfamiliar modern repeating rifles. The cannon ammunition had to be tested, producing another rodeo for the scouts and their still skittish horses. Strange was certain additional ammunition would be required for the cannon, so a group of volunteers, including two local women—Mrs. Sutter and Mrs. Mitchell—volunteered to make up bags of lead balls and gunpowder charges. These were to supplement the 150 rounds Colonel Perry was bringing with the cannon and for the antique armament from Fort Edmonton's armoury.

Strange called Steele to his command tent for another discussion about his plan of splitting the force: one part of the force floating down the river and the rest marching east, across land on the Victoria trail. He queried Sam's past experience of the Fort Pitt area, which he'd been through on two previous occasions: on the original march west and during the signing of Treaty Number Six as well as during patrol work when he was stationed in Edmonton in the mid-1870s. Sam agreed Jingo's plan was feasible because the paddlewheel steamboats regularly plied the river so the scows shouldn't encounter serious difficulties with the springtime high water. The Victoria trail was well used now, not the nearly indiscernible track it had been just a few years previously, and would also be useful for future transport wagon trains that would provide supplies to the force. He believed the column could travel down it with few serious difficulties, provided they weren't attacked by hostiles.

Strange required eight wooden scows for the water-borne force, which they either had constructed or purchased. These were flat-bottomed barge-type vessels of varying sizes. The construction consisted of a double layer of rough-sawn planks, pinned together with wooden pegs rather than nails—a feature that gave the hulls flexibility. Flexible construction allowed the vessel better survivability when it ran aground, which was a common occurrence in river travel on the North Saskatchewan. The disadvantage was they tended to leak water profusely despite the caulking, thus requiring almost constant bailing until the wood absorbed enough water to swell up and close the gaps. The lead scow of the fleet was fitted out with the nine-pound (weight of the projectile) cannon from Fort Macleod. They lashed the gun carriage to the bow so that it faced forward; therefore, when the gun was fired the whole boat could absorb the recoil. It was aimed left and right by turning the scow in the river current with long oars called sweeps, and the

River Scow, 1900.
Scows were used as transportation long after the rebellion concluded.
Strange's scows featured higher sides than this one.

Section of Pork & flour-clad for Infantry

River Scow Crossection Diagram.
Sketched by General Strange, indicating how supplies
were used as fortification in the event of an attack.

elevation was adjusted by a screw jack that moved the barrel up and down. This combination, though crude, would bring the gun to bear on its target. This barge was technically the first and only "battleship" ever to ply the waters of Alberta or Saskatchewan and was aptly named *Big Bear*. (The *Northcote* paddlewheeler used at Batoche was defended with only small arms.)

Five barges carried the militia along with the police gun team and the wagon drivers. They were protected along the sides by stacks of supplies and equipment and dubbed, "Flour Clad." The troops christened three as *Nancy*, *Bauset*, and *Roy du Bord*. Each of the scows had "battlestations" created by gaps in the supplies or by loopholes cut into the hull's sides. These stations were manned by the better militia marksmen who poked their rifles through the holes in readiness of fending off an attack should they drift into a trap. The last scow was newly built and used to transport the six horses of the cannon and caisson, but was the worst of them all for leakage. This barge had hay bale protection around the sides, thus earning the name "Hay Clad." They also acquired a ferry, complete with its cable and capstan, from Clover Bar. Strange anticipated using it at Fort Pitt when they arrived to facilitate moving troops quickly across the river. All these vessels were propelled primarily by the flow of the river with the sweeps or oars; a rudder rigged at the stern provided manoeuvrability in the current. None of the scows sat more than a metre deep in the water when fully loaded.

The commanding officer of the Winnipeg Light Infantry was shocked at Strange's planned use of the flotilla. After viewing and inspecting the scows nearing completion he lodged an official protest with Strange, condemning the construction. The use of flour and hay for armour was to his mind absurd and he officially demanded a board of inquiry. Despite these protests the boats were eventually declared "fit," and the WLI was the first to disembark from them after floating on the river downstream.

Steele and the scouts were ready to begin their march east from Fort Edmonton on the morning of May 6. The scouts were to shepherd some supply wagons, spare horses, and the remainder of the 65th Mount Royal Rifles along the trail to the Victoria settlement—a distance of about 70 kilometres. At the last minute the wagon teamsters refused to go unless they were provided with guns. A report of an Indian attack at the Victoria settlement had thoroughly unnerved the drivers who believed to proceed without a firearm was sheer folly. The situation was difficult to resolve since no rifles were available locally, and the supply column with the additional armament had not yet arrived. Strange felt an urgency to move east, so waiting for the supplies was out of the question. A compromise was achieved by a promise that the rifles would be issued at Victoria, where the column would re-unite, prior to proceeding any further.

Steele finally left Fort Edmonton with his scouts in the lead, and on each flank of the two companies of the 65th under Captain Prevost were the supply wagons and spare horses. As Steele led his column eastward he couldn't help remembering the mind-numbing, exhausting duty he'd experienced some ten years previously as part of Inspector Jarvis's column, stumbling their way along on the last part of the "Great March," the NWMP's initial trek from Fort Dufferin to Fort Edmonton. On that epic journey they had used the southern trail a few miles away across the river. He occasionally glanced ruefully in that direction as the recollection of events flooded back into his mind.

Milton Williams, a trooper in the volunteer contingent of the scouts, later related an incident that illustrates how nervous the force was as it penetrated hostile territory of the Cree near today's Waskatenau:

> "The trails as a rule were bad with so many sloughs and creeks to cross, and as it was spring the creeks were usually running full. We were travelling through densely wooded country, a good place for the Indians to attack us we thought. We came to a small stream, harmless to look at, but awful to cross. The first part of the column had got through but the banks became slippery from mud and water dripping off the horses and wagons.[9]
>
> While the 65th was trying to get one of the last wagons through we heard a shout from the officer directing the work, 'Send back for the rear guard!' (the trailing scouts). Immediate panic occurred amongst the scouts and they came rushing past, mud and water flying, forcing their way to the front shouting as they went, 'Clear the road!' We listened for the reports of

Milton Williams,
Steele's Scout.
Milton (seen here in 1917,
right, with his family) was
the author of a very
descriptive letter of events
during the march from
Edmonton to Fort Pitt.

the carbines, but none came. Finally we began to think that possibly there were no Indians at the front to fight. Soon the horsemen came splashing back, laughing and joking as they passed. There'd be no 'fun' that day."[10]

The mistake happened when the 65th's officer had called for his militia rear guard to help pull the wagon through the creek. The scouts heard his call and thought Steele—at the head of the column—had met some hostiles, so they instantly rushed to his aid in expectation of a skirmish.

The very next day another incident happened that proved embarrassing for the scouts although no harm was done. Again, Milton Williams related the fiasco in a letter:

"The day was hot, no breeze at all and we were close to the banks of the North Saskatchewan. We began to wish it was dinner time and shortly found a suitable spot and waited for Major Steele to come up and order a halt. We heard a horse coming through the bush, headed

Victoria Settlement.
A post rebellion shooting competition.

straight for us. The rider was bare-headed, his eyes wide
with fright and excitement. He was bootless, as well as
hatless and there was no saddle on the horse. The rider
carried a double-barrelled shotgun which he beat the
horse with, all the time kicking it in the ribs 200 strokes
a minute. He rode up to the Major and excitedly told of
being chased by Indians only a few minutes before. Major
Steele listened quietly and calmly, putting a question or
two so as to get some information clear enough to make
a judgement. A force was quickly made up, Captain
Oswald in command and along with a half breed guide
(from Edmonton) started to follow the track of the
enemy. They soon sighted some carts and horses on the
trail ahead but no men. The boys began to prepare for
action, loading their guns, tightening their saddles and
locating extra ammunition. We rode past the carts and
horses and located footprints where men had gone into
the bush. After a time we had worked our way in a circle
back to the trail and found more, clearer tracks. Upon
examination the tracks proved to be those of our own
advanced guard!" [Coryell's group][11]

Strange felt a preliminary scouting of the trail was necessary prior to the militia column's advance. He considered the scouting duty was so dangerous that the use of regular scouts was out of the question. He called on the man who he felt had the best chance of succeeding in the risky assignment, the Reverend George McKay. He outlined the situation with "the fighting preacher," saying, "Now remember, I am not ordering you to make this ride. From the last reports I have received, it would be a case of cold-blooded murder on my part to order you on such an errand, but if you undertake it on your own initiative you will be doing a great service for your force and your country."[12]

McKay considered the request for only a moment and confidently replied, "I will make the ride and I will go well armed. If you do not hear from me within reasonable time, you may take it for granted that I have been killed by the Indians. Rest assured they will never take me prisoner alive as long as I have a cartridge left."[13]

Later that same day McKay, alone, far ahead of the column and west of Victoria, noticed three Indians walking along the trail in the distance. As he silently studied their progress he thought to himself, "Might as well have a skirmish, maybe even capture them." He manoeuvred his horse closer, quietly moving along a game trail that intersected the path they were using. The three had their rifles unexpectedly slung over their shoulders making McKay's intention somewhat safer for him as he prepared his surprise. As the three made their way along the ridge they came within a couple of metres of the silent waiting preacher. At the opportune moment McKay charged into the open with his rifle ready. "Naki. Pakitina!" ("Halt. Put it down!") He shouted in Cree. The surprise worked to his advantage and the three instantly dropped their rifles on the ground. McKay collected the firearms and marched them at gunpoint back to the main force as they followed up his trail. That evening they were shackled to iron balls and placed in a guarded tent.

One of the three was probably Windyboy from Saddle Lake. The reserve's folklore tells how he escaped from the guarded tent at night, and despite carrying a 48-kilogram ball and chain shackled to his foot, eluded capture and returned to Saddle Lake. With the help of other warriors he was able to get the encumbrance off his leg and dispose of it in a nearby slough to sink forever out of sight. Several days later, fearing recapture, he left his family and the reserve, travelling south through Hobbema to the Rockyboy Reserve in Montana, never to return. He was a younger brother of Meminook, whom Steele was to fatefully encounter a couple of weeks later.

When Steele's Scouts rode into Victoria, the settlement was in utter turmoil. A few weeks previously a feeble attack by Saddle Lake Indians was repulsed, and now men were again running to the inadequate fortifications while children were herded indoors by ashen-faced women. As Steele rode up in his red tunic, the men shouted to him that an Indian attack was imminent. Steele had his men frantically search the bush of the valley for two hours without finding a trace of the Indians. They eventually came to the realization that two young boys from the settlement, out for a ride on their ponies, had encountered Steele's advance scouts who were dressed in buckskin jackets. Unfortunately the scouts called out to the boys "Tcheskwa, pitama!" ("Wait a minute!" in Cree.) The young fellows, thinking that they had encountered Indians, understandably panicked and rode for the settlement as hard as the ponies would go to spread the warning.

Unknown to General Strange, on May 12, the Métis stronghold of Batoche had been overrun by Middleton's troops in a daring, spontaneous charge, led by Colonel Williams. The Métis were routed, and on May 15, Louis Riel surrendered, ending the Métis rebellion, but not the fighting. Big Bear had yet to be dealt with as he still held the captives from Frog Lake and Fort Pitt.

Strange's flotilla drifted away from the Edmonton landing on May 14, led by the scouts paddling canoes ahead, checking the shoreline for activity as they went. A second group of scouts rode along the river valley with the same task. Near Fort Saskatchewan the "Hayclad" barge with the horses on board temporarily sank at the south shore. The crew failed with their bailing effort to keep ahead of the leaking problem and the scow settled to the shallow bottom, full of water. The horses were led off the submerged vessel and taken across the river to join the land column. The scow was re-floated and towed along empty for the rest of the way to Fort Pitt. In the evening the boats were tied to trees on shore, and the men slept on board while sentries were extended up the hillside. The mounted scouts patrolled the perimeter as usual. Another spring sleet storm came up and continued most of the next day, making conditions, once again, utterly miserable for the force. The French culture of the Edmonton Métis came to the fore as these boatmen—faced with the adversity—began to sing their way downstream, ignoring the cold blustery weather. Strange didn't have the heart to quiet them, deciding there was little harm in their enthusiasm, possibly even a benefit by showing any prowling Indian they were confident in their duty. The singing naturally tailed off toward evening on its own accord as the risk of attack increased. The flotilla arrived at Victoria settlement on May 16. The barges were anchored to the north shore at the landing and camp was set up adjacent to the settlement.

On a picturesque flat by the North Saskatchewan River, the Hudson's Bay Company had erected a fur trade post in 1864, naming it Victoria. The fortification had not been maintained, yet over the years the settlement expanded along the north bank of the river. Now Strange surveyed the scattered buildings that remained and ordered a clean-up and improvement of the defences. For the next few days fortifications were improved; then it was again foot drill on the parade square and rifle practice for the militia and the scouts who weren't out on patrol.

On the rim of the North Saskatchewan River valley stood three men surveying the valley before them. Below, next to the river on a flat, sprawled a military camp with the British Union Jack fluttering on the pole in a parade square neatly bordered by white tents aligned in rows. Soldiers in red moved about the green grass, while in the distance an ominous grey-black cloudbank contrasted with the blue of the springtime sky overhead. The scene was the fulfillment of Peter Shirt's vision. Peter was an adopted son of Peter Erasmus, the bulbous-nosed trader and interpreter, employed by the Indians for the signing of Treaty Number Six in 1876 at Fort Carlton and a later co-signing at Fort Pitt. With them stood James Senium, better known as Chief Pakan of the Whitefish Lake Cree, who lived about 50 kilometres north of Victoria. They had come, because of Shirt's vision, to pledge their alliance and friendship with the soldiers of their great white mother, the Queen.

About a year previous, Peter Shirt had experienced a dream or vision in which a spirit came to him in the form of an old man, took him by the hand, and told him to look to the east. Peter envisioned tumultuous, dark, stormy clouds with flashing lightning and deafening thunder. The old man then told him to turn and look to the west. As Peter responded he saw before him rows of red-coated soldiers and white tents. Shirt was confused and asked what it meant, and received the reply, "Great harm may come to your people Peter. Heed my warning!" He then asked the old man when this would come to pass. The reply was, "When the white horse dies." It made no sense to Peter since he didn't have a white horse. He sought out his adopted father, Peter Erasmus, told him of the vision, and asked what he thought it meant. Erasmus couldn't shed any light on the vision's meaning, but he advised not to forget the dream for it surely was of importance. Over the ensuing time Erasmus did acquire a white horse through a trade, and in February of 1885 it became trapped in deep snow and subsequently died.

After the Frog Lake massacre in April, emissaries came to the reserve from Big Bear's band trying to convince Chief Pakan to join in the uprising against the whites. Shirt, hearing of the council meeting planned for that night, suddenly recollected his dream and went to Erasmus, to convince him that they must attend the council's sitting. At the gathering Shirt recounted his vision, with Erasmus vouching for it and the fact the white horse was indeed dead. Pakan took the omen to heart and ultimately refused to join the resistance. One of the emissaries, Louis Cardinal, was shot and killed the following day and Pakan, fearing reprisal from Big Bear's warriors or Cardinal's family,

James Seenum (Chief Pakan).
Pakan was chief of the Whitefish Lake
Cree and a participant in the legend
of Peter Shirt's dream.

Winnipeg Light Infantry.
The Indians saw the WLI, dressed in red tunics, as representatives of the Queen and held a subservient respect for them. General Strange captialized on this by ordering the WLI to march overland from Victoria settlement to Fort Pitt, clearly displaying their authority.

fled with his band into the bush southwest of Whitefish Lake. Shirt, Erasmus, and Seenum (Pakan) then travelled to the Victoria settlement with the intention of seeking refuge for the band under the white missionary's protection.

As these three men stood gazing down in awe on the settlement and the militia camp, Peter Shirt, with tears streaming down his face muttered, "My dream, it was of a war with the whites and I know now our people will be destroyed!" Peter Shirt's vision had come true!

Suddenly they were startled by the sound of a Winchester rifle's action click as a cartridge was chambered behind them. One of Steele's Scouts had been watching the approach of the three and silently slipped up unnoticed behind them. At gunpoint the scout marched them down the hill toward the camp and in front of General Strange. Chief Pakan promised his band's alliance with Strange's militia but refused to have any of his people act as guides. His intent was to remain friendly, but neutral. It was fortunate Whitefish Lake and Saddle Lake Indians generally abstained from the insurrection that was centred east of Victoria. Had they joined in hostilities with Big Bear and Poundmaker, the Beaver Lake Cree near Lac La Biche would surely have merged in the hostilities as well. This in turn may well have spread in a snowball

The Alberta Field Force on the March.
*Transport wagons cross a muskeg. Steele's Scouts are in
the right foreground. The rebellion occurred during
a wet, rainy spring, hampering progress*

effect with band after band joining the rebellion and possibly causing a
bloody and fruitless war through all of the Alberta territory.

☆ ☆ ☆

General Strange decided to reverse the marching order of the militia,
and because of the newspaper correspondents accompanying them, he
held the change to the last moment. Jingo had reason to believe this
press information sent with the scout couriers would be published in
the Winnipeg newspaper. This news would get to the Métis at Batoche,
and in turn back to the Indians, which he would face in the near future.
The 65th Mount Royal Rifles would ride in the barges on the river and
the Winnipeg Light Infantry, whose uniforms resembled the NWMP,
representative of the Queen, would march by land.

On May 17, Steele and his scouts led the WLI, wagons and horses,
out of Victoria. They marched along the established trail above the
river valley toward Saddle Lake. Lieutenant Coryell led the advance
group, at times aggressively ranging out some 40 kilometres into hostile
territory. While on this reconnaissance from the column they
discovered a cache of stolen supplies hidden by some of the Saddle
Lake Indians who were sympathizers of Big Bear. They had stashed

the spoils of a trading post raid in expectation of general warfare erupting in the area as it had at Fort Pitt. Coryell's determined scouting caused some concern for Steele when they failed to report in to him for two days. Steele began to imagine, needlessly, that they had been ambushed and possibly wiped out by hostiles.

On May 19, the skies opened up again and a downpour lasting for the whole day turned the trail into a muddy morass churned up by the wagons and horses, so the following militia struggled along almost knee deep in churned up black ooze. Despite Sergeant Borradaile's diligent trail improvement work, progress of the land force was slower than that of the flotilla who left Victoria on May 20. Almost one full day was used to rebuild a bridge at the creek crossing just south of Saddle Lake. When the column advanced eastward, the flat, more open country became drier and easier to travel and the troops increased their pace again as a result.

Messenger scouts commuting between Steele's land column and the flotilla maintained communication. This was risky work, galloping alone through unknown, hostile country between the two forces. Sam's brothers, Richard and Godfrey, were able to contrive temporary leave to join the force and later caught up with the land column near Victoria. On May 22 Strange mentioned that one of them was able to display a bullet hole through his hat after being shot at while carrying messages near Saddle Lake. The trail Steele followed passed by the south shore of Saddle Lake and continued due east along the telegraph line and what is now the main street of St. Paul. A few kilometres farther east, it veered southeast along the creek toward Elk Point and the old fort site of Dog Rump House, upstream from the river bridge. During this portion of the march incessant rain continued to fall, and yet the force marched an astounding 55 kilometres in one long, hard day.

On the night of May 22, the scouts were patrolling just below the valley top when an unseen Indian sniper took several shots at the barges tied up on the riverbank, just upstream from today's Duverney, described by Strange as "St. Pauls" (St. Paul de Cris). The 65th hurriedly disembarked; the excited soldiers stormed through the riverbank bush in skirmish order, returning a random fire at the unseen sniper. Above them the bewildered land-bound scouts had to take cover in a ravine to escape the flying bullets that whistled past them. The instigator of the incident was never located despite the probing of the 65th. From that day on the militia disembarked from the tied-up scows each night to bivouac on shore rather than remaining vulnerable on the vessels resting in water.

Jingo Strange commented on the country they were passing through:

> "The character of the country continued the same from Victoria undulating and intersected by creeks, lakes and swamps draining into the Saskatchewan, varied by thickly wooded poplar bluffs, interspersed with open patches of prairie. The soil was a rich black vegetable mould, doubtless very fertile if cultivated, but there were no signs of such since leaving Victoria, except the patch of farm cultivated for the Indians near Saddle and Frog Lake Reserves."

Strange decided it was imperative that he establish communications with Colonel Otter at Battleford, who in turn was in contact with General Middleton. He asked for volunteers to take a canoe downstream, through dangerous Indian-controlled country, with messages and reports of his progress to the eastern forces. Sergeant Borradaile, possibly tiring of the construction detail and hoping for some excitement in this great adventure, volunteered along with William Scott, a scout from Calgary. They were to hide out in the riverbank bush during the day and paddle at night down the North Saskatchewan River to Battleford. They succeeded in completing this harrowing trip despite nearly drowning when they overturned their canoe as they came into shore early one morning to hide. Borradaile's sidearm came out of its holster when they were thrashing around in the water retrieving their supplies and was lost during the incident.

Middleton had by then defeated the Métis at Batoche and was now camped at Battleford. Borradaile reported directly to the General and requested another pistol to replace the lost one at the same time. Middleton bluntly refused, telling Borradaile, "A big stick is sufficient protection for your return journey." The disgusted sergeant/scout returned upriver, without a sidearm, rejoining Strange's force at Fort Pitt, and printed on his upturned hat brim were the disgruntled words, "I was *not* at Fish Creek! I was *not* at Batoche!"

Frog Lake Settlement, 1885.
Captain Rutherford's sketch of the burnt Hudson's Bay stores.

Same Location as Seen Today.
The location of the above scene is approximately 300 metres east of monument. (The photo's angle required the use of a stepladder to attain a similar perspective to Rutherford's sketch, indicating the captain probably made the sketch from horseback.)

The flotilla drifted past the old fort sites of White Earth and D' Isle, bivouacking on May 23 downstream from Dog Rump Creek and the old trading post that was once located there. Major Hatton and the remainder of the Alberta Mounted Rifles, who had finally caught up to the main force, joined them. They spent the night, once again with the rain pounding on the tents, lying in wet clothing and blankets on soggy ground.

The next day, Sunday, was the Queen's birthday and the occasion demanded a general address by Strange to the entire force despite the continuing rain. The ranks assembled and the general jumped onto the back of a wagon to address the already soggy men standing before him "at ease" in orderly rows:

> "Colonel Smith, officers, and men of the Light Infantry. You have marched admirably, and I am proud of the stuff I command. This is the Queen's birthday, without the Queen's weather. We cannot have any fireworks to-day, Mr. Big Bear won't give us the chance, but from information I have, we are close behind him, and when the chance does come, I know you are the stuff to take it. As this is the Queen's birthday, let us give her three cheers!"[14]

The force was on the move again, marching or floating in the scows past the Fort George and Buckingham House ruins of some 80 years previous. Later in the afternoon the sun finally showed itself and the thankful men dried out and warmed up as they continued moving eastward.

They arrived at the mouth of Frog Creek where it joins the North Saskatchewan, and bivouacked for the night on the flat area just downstream of the creek. Lieutenant Coryell and a detail of scouts were deployed to the Frog Lake settlement where a few of the ruins still smouldered. They searched the ruins and found the charred remains of the two priests in what was left of the church. Their dismembered bodies would have been unrecognizable except for their prayer beads. The men were forced to wear rum-soaked bandanas over their faces in order to retrieve the priests' remains for burial. William Parker, one of the detail men, found the sight horrifying despite his police experience. He discovered young Gilchrist's decomposing body lying face down on the ground not far from his shack, his mouth jammed full of dirt and grass. He suspected Gilchrist had reacted to the pain of the fatal wounds, biting the ground as he lay dying.

The bodies were removed and buried alongside the other markers in the church graveyard where they remain today. Presiding over the burial service was Reverend McKay, having temporarily exchanged his guns for a Bible. Upon returning, the men of the burial party were given the "freedom of the camp" for the rest of the day in recognition of their dour duty. Later that evening after supper some of the officers of the militia walked up to the settlement to see for themselves the carnage that had occurred over a month and a half previously. Most could only shake their heads in disgust and resentment as they walked about the ruins, viewing the carnage.

In the meantime, members of the 65th Mount Royal Rifles requested and received permission to erect a seventeen-metre-tall cross on the hill above camp and to bury a document commemorating the memory of the Frog Lake Massacre victims. That evening a cross and message were prepared with the following inscription carved in the bark:

ERECTED
in memory of the victims
of
FROG LAKE
by the 65th Battalion
May 24, 1885

At 5:00 a.m. after breakfast the men climbed the hill, held a short prayer service, and completed their task. They christened the hill where the cairn was located as "Mont-Croix." Records indicate the message in the capsule simply states:

"D.O.M."
"This cross was erected on Pentecost Sunday, the 24th of May 1885 by the officers, N.C.O.s and soldiers of the 3rd, 4th, 5th, and 6th Companies of the 65 Battalion, C.M.R., under the command of Lieutenant-Colonel G.A. Hughes, Brigade Major, and in the

memory of the Oblate Fathers and other victims who
were massacred by the Indians at Frog Lake on the 2nd
of April, 1885.
Signed by all the Officers of the 65th."[15]

That day Captain Oswald, leading the advance scouting party, sent
a messenger back to Jingo advising that "the Indians were still around
the Fort Pitt area in strength." Strange immediately ordered the cannon
and caisson off the barge, and along with Steele's Scouts and the cannon's
gun team, rode ahead of the Winnipeg Light Infantry on the trail to Fort
Pitt, arriving in the evening without sighting the enemy but in time to
discover yet another grizzly scene.

They crested the river valley on the trail that led down towards the
fort. On the ground before them was sprawled the stripped and mutilated
body of Constable David Cowan with the decaying carcass of his horse
beside him. Impaled on a stick near the corpse were the shrivelled
remains of the young policeman's heart. A burial detail was ordered
and a grave dug near a narrow ravine to the north of the fort, not far
from where the Treaty Number Six signing ceremonies were held nine
years before.

The next morning, a full dress service was conducted by Canon
McKay and was attended by his police comrades and the commanding
militia officers. Afterwards, the police constructed a small willow fence
and positioned it around the grave. According to Reverend McKay, these
two recent and repugnant discoveries caused the entire force to have
the mental attitude to seek retribution at the earliest moment.

Anticipating a possible attack, Strange posted orders for the
remaining unburned buildings of the fort to be cleaned out and
rudimentary fortifications constructed to make it as defensible as
possible. These were to be constantly improved over the next few weeks
by militia work parties but were never to be put to the test. The end of
Fort Pitt as an active major trade centre would be heralded by the
conclusion of the rebellion.

"Mont-Croix" on the North Saskatchewan River.
*Wayne Brown, the author, in 1996 at the site where the 65th Mount
Royal Rifles erected a cross to commemorate the victims of the Frog Lake
Massacre. They also buried a "time capsule" at the foot of the cross.*

Frog Lake Massacre Monument and Graves.
*The graves of the massacre victims lie in two neat rows. Constable David
Cowan's body rests beside them. His body was exumed from Fort Pitt and
moved to this location for the dedication of this monument on June 9, 1925.*

With the flotilla drifting down the North Saskatchewan River, Steele and the land force left Edmonton following the trail from Jasper Avenue eastward along Victoria Trail to opposite Fort Saskatchewan, where the old North West Company's Fort Augustus was located. From there they continued, following the telegraph line, passing just south of Redwater, Waskatenau, around the river bend, and down to Victoria Settlement, which is south of Smoky Lake. This settlement has been re-constructed and an interpretive centre established approximately five kilometres downstream from the Highway #855 bridge.

From Victoria the force continued toward Saddle Lake, still following the telegraph line and using the trail that is now Highway #652, on to St. Paul where the trail evolved into the main street of the town. From here it went eastward about ten kilometres, crossed Dog Rump Creek, then followed the east side of the drainage to their bivouac located at the Elk Point bridge on Highway #41. Fort White Earth, a trading post of the late 1700s, was located at the confluence of White Earth Creek and the river. Fort D' Isle is located halfway down an island about three kilometres downstream from the Highway bridge on #881. Here the fur-trading fort of the X Y Company that put Fort George and Buckingham House out of business at the turn of the eighteenth century still lies virtually undisturbed after nearly two hundred years. A cairn marks its location on the north side of the island. Fort George and Buckingham House are located about ten kilometres east of Elk Point; this historical location features a new interpretative centre.

The Frog Lake monument and grave markers that are dedicated to the massacre victims are located about three kilometres east of the Frog Lake Post Office and store on Highway #897. The basement of the church is a few metres to the west of the monument, poorly marked, and engulfed by the bush. Some of the other basements of the original buildings can be located to the east of the monument and they are also poorly marked and completely neglected. Of interest is recent electronic investigation that indicates there are more graves at the monument than indicated by the crosses. Unpublished records indicate there may be at least twelve massacre victims! Research continues on this aspect of the massacre.

The bivouac sight at Frog Creek is located on posted, private land west of Highway #897, south of Frog Lake and off the end of Township Road #552. Around 1990, a group of local history buffs re-discovered the location and unearthed the capsule planted by the 65th in 1885. A replica cross made from poplar trees was erected by the group at the site. The capsule is still unopened and temporarily with the Alberta Museum in Edmonton. The intention is to return it to the local museum once it's permanently established.

Fort Pitt is located approximately three kilometres south of Secondary Highway #797 east of the Alberta-Saskatchewan boundary. There is a commemorative cairn with descriptive signage at the location and nearby is a reproduction of one of the main buildings of the fort, constructed over fifty years ago by the landowner. The cut made for the sternwheeler riverboat landing and subsequent ferry is still visible. The trail Constable Cowan, Constable Loasby, and scout Quinn fatefully rode in their desperate attempt at seeking safety is not visible but lies just a few metres south of and parallel to a field road coming down the hill, which is used daily by the Hutterite brethren in their farming pursuits. This piece of land surrounding the fort reeks with history. "Pitt" was built from timbers that were originally part of Dog Rump House at Elk Point in 1829. Fort Pitt was also the second site after Fort Carlton for the co-signing of Treaty Number Six in 1876. The location for this ceremony was just south of a drainage ravine, on a plateau of land over the crest of the hill looking westward. Sam Steele was present at both the Carlton and Pitt signing ceremonies. General Strange's Alberta Field Force camp was located on this same plateau about a kilometre north of the fort, which places it above the bend in the river.

Frog Lake Massacre Memorial.
A consulting company using what was described to the author as "ground sensing radar" to determine the location of decreased remains at Frog Lake Massacre Memorial. The unit indicated more bodies than grave markers, which supports stories that there were more than nine killed that day as detailed in official records. (Two were supposed to be bootlegging Metis, who were "conveniently removed" for their bad dealings, and a Native woman, and possibly her child.)

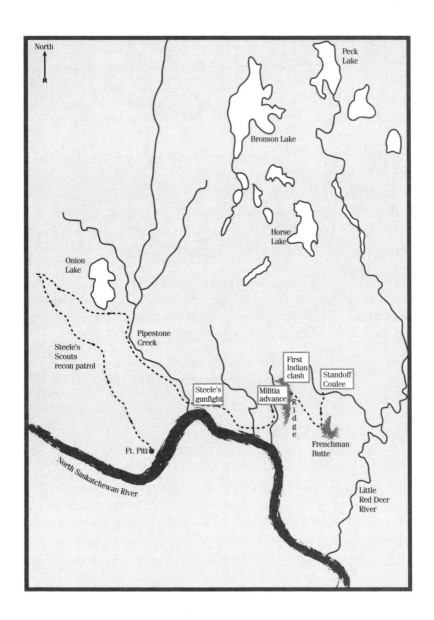

North

Peck Lake

Bronson Lake

Horse Lake

Onion Lake

Pipestone Creek

Steele's Scouts recon patrol

First Indian clash

Standoff Coulee

Steele's gunfight

Militia advance

Ridge

Ft. Pitt

Frenchman Butte

North Saskatchewan River

Little Red Deer River

Chapter 5

SEARCHING FOR THE REBELS

Steele's Scouts, along with the militia of the Alberta Field Force, made Fort Pitt their temporary headquarters, setting up camp north of the fort's burned-out ruins on a plateau above the river flat. From here there was a view eastward into hostile territory, straight down the North Saskatchewan River for about fifteen kilometres. They were also a little more exposed to the wind so the horses and men didn't suffer quite so much from the pestilent mosquitoes and flies. On May 26, General Strange ordered two patrols of scouts to locate the Indians that Captain Oswald had earlier reported in the area. They reconnoitred a short distance around the fort on the south side of the river, finding only meagre signs of Indian presence along the Battleford trail.

Later that morning Sam discovered a folded letter lying on the ground several kilometres north of the fort. When he opened it he instantly recognized its writer as Miss Amelia McLean. It had been sent to her mother from St. John's Ladies' College in Winnipeg, the very paper she'd proudly shown him during his visit with them five years previous. This confirmed for him that she was an Indian prisoner not far away, and he fretted for her and her family's safety.

During the mid-afternoon of May 26, a scout discovered a heavily travelled trail going northward. Steele reported to General Strange, "Sir, my scouts have found a well-used Indian trail which indicates they have travelled north, possibly to Onion Lake. I think that despite not being fresh, it's worth following up."

Fort Pitt, 1884.
*Looking east toward Fort Pitt, the Battleford trail climbs the river
valley in the background. Constance Cowan was killed somewhere
behind the photographer's position.*

Strange's interest was peaked. "Definitely, Steele. Take as many
scouts as you can and determine where the trail leads, but don't attack
them. Any scrap we have with them should be decisive and surely you'd
likely be badly outnumbered."

A few minutes later several newspaper reporters attached to the
force noticed the preparations of the scouts and discovered their
mission. The reporters had just finished a conversation with a few of
the scouts who had returned from a foray south of the river, where
they speculated the Indians would go. The conjecture was the Cree
would make for the Battleford area to unite with Chief Poundmaker's
band. The reporters immediately stomped up to the general and a
heated argument broke out. One reporter, on the verge of shouting
exclaimed, "I know damn well the Indians would go to Battleford. It's
only logical. And besides, I think Steele is crazy to think they'd go
north, way into the bush!"

Steele joined the group and firmly stated, "I'm confident we've
located the trail. It is heavily used by wagons, horses, and by natives

Fort Pitt, Today.
Monument, descriptive plaques, and a re-constructed building are all that remain of a once bustling fur trading post. This photo was taken from the same position as the 1884 photo.

walking. And I've also found a letter, which was written by one of the captives. I believe the trail on the south side is of only a few Indians. My scout claims the prints of one of them is a female native wearing shoes, not moccasins. From the tracks she has no experience with her footwear, and I'm convinced the Indians went north!"

Jingo Strange, confident in Steele's unerring judgement, told the group Steele would continue as previously ordered, and he was to leave immediately. In consolation to the complaining reporters and sensitive to their potential newspaper writings Strange ordered Inspector A. Bowen Perry to take his police, Reverend McDougall, and Canon McKay, cross the river and search there.

With that agreeable direction Steele left Strange's command tent and rushed back to where his scouts were now mounted and waiting. Perry too was convinced Steele was right and expressed his bitterness at not being able to go where the action was sure to be. However he obeyed his orders and reluctantly took twenty of the police scouts, which included his trained cannon team from Fort Macleod, and crossed the river on the now operational ferry. In just nineteen hours, he found himself within kilometres of Battleford. He continued on to the fort despite Strange's orders not to venture past a well-known fork part way along the south trail. His orders seemed to be in conflict, specifically that he should establish contact with General Middleton if it were feasible, yet not to continue past the fork. He succeeded in reporting to the general, but despite Perry's vehement objections, Middleton ordered him to remain at Battleford and return to Fort Pitt along with his main force. Perry and these members of the police scouts thereby missed out on the historic action to come. The wait consumed over a week of their valuable time before they were to see Fort Pitt.

Sam shouted the order, "Follow me!" and led his column of two officers and 90 men out of Fort Pitt, up the hill, and westward on the trail to Onion Lake. Steele and the scouts made a circuitous route up through Onion Lake and the small settlement there, then eastward to the Pipestone Creek and back south toward the river where a crossing existed just above its confluence with the North Saskatchewan. With the late, wet spring, the creek was nearly in full flood and there would surely be signs of a large group having crossed since they were pulling packed carts and wagons of supplies, teepees, and spoils from the looted trading posts and "Pitt."

Sam halted his column of scouts on the crest of the Saskatchewan River valley. There was an ominous feeling in the air as he looked up the valley to see the campfires of Strange's force clearly evident "about three miles to the west."

A Chipewyan Indian guide quietly warned, "I can smell Indians!"

Heeding the guide's comment, Steele left the column at the top of the valley in command of Captain Coryell. He chose Joseph Butlin and Thomas McClelland to accompany him; then the trio carefully headed their horses down the slope into the river valley. Steele's plan was that James Oswald and William Wright would follow a short distance behind as a rear guard for them. It was now past eleven o'clock under an inky dark, moonless, overcast sky. They'd found nothing so far on the long ride, and the men and horses were dead tired; it was time to bivouac and rest.

The trio's horses were virtually noiseless as they stealthily covered the damp, soft ground. Steele surveyed the area in the darkness. In a low tone he remarked, "This is just the thing!" when suddenly there was a brilliant flash of fire from a rifle to his front right and a deafening bang! A bullet zinged past his face—another flash and bang!—a second bullet hissed by, putting a hole in his tunic sleeve. The startled horses reared and jumped as the three men desperately tried to bring their already drawn guns to bear.

Meminook, the Indian who fired at Sam, jumped from a patch of tall prairie grass and dashed across in front of the scouts' horses to his own pony on Steele's left. Just as the native slipped onto the back of his black horse McClelland brought the sights of his Winchester into alignment in the dark and snapped a telling shot. His bullet penetrated the Indian's neck, instantly killing him before Steele could fire his Adams revolver.

Sam saw the silhouette of another Indian on a horse 28 metres away at the edge of the trees, aiming a rifle at him. Another flash and bang! He, too, missed. Steele ineffectively snapped a shot back at the shadow with his pistol.

The whole area instantly erupted with whooping, yelling Indians as they burst from the trees and brush on their ponies! McClelland and Butlin, with their adrenalin pumping added to the frenzy: shouting, swearing, firing, and reloading as fast as they could. Despite the close quarters of the gunfight neither side was effective because of the blinding effect the muzzle flashes had on their eyesight in the dark.

Sam later described the close quarters of the wild gunfight: "The hot flashes from the Winchester's of the Indians almost singed our faces, and several times we had to pause lest we shoot one another." The fierce firefight went on for almost a full minute, clearly heard by the pensive sentries on duty all the way back at Fort Pitt. The Indians dashed past the firing scouts helter-skelter toward the east, past Steele's rear guard of Oswald and Wright, who, in turn urged them on with a few inaccurate shots of their own.

It was deathly quiet after the Indian ponies' pounding hooves faded away in the distance. Steele carefully checked the body of Meminook while the others probed the nearby trees for possible lingering wounded warriors until Captain Coryell arrived with the rest of the column to join them. Anticipating another attack Steele ordered the scouts to set up a defensive perimeter and to build protection from fallen logs, then to lay silently in readiness of the Indians' return. After about two hours

Sam Steele's Midnight Gunfight, Pipestone Creek.
Sketch made "after the fact" by General T. B. Strange. Meminook (left),
fired first while crossing in front of Steele (facing the artist). McClelland
(centre) and Butlin (dismounted) spring to action as more Indians on
horseback burst out from hiding.

Pipestone Creek Crossing Today, Looking West.
Carlton trail is visible passing through the fence. The gunfight
probably occurred on the left, just out of the photo. Fort Pitt is
at the bend of the valley, just above the fence gate.

a wet drizzle began to fall, and the time until dawn was spent in nervous apprehension, Winchesters at the ready, lying on the sodden ground, waiting for an attack that never came.

At first light Steele sent a messenger back to "Pitt" to inform General Strange of the encounter and his intention to follow the retreating Indians east. Strange instantly mobilized his force, broke camp, and began a forced march with his main force of Winnipeg Light Infantry toward Steele's pensively bivouacked scouts. The 65th Mount Royal Rifles were ordered into the scows to float downstream in support of the ground force.

About two weeks later the *Calgary Bulletin*, a predecessor of the *Calgary Herald*, printed the following article:

Joe Butlin to the Fore

The honour of being the first man of Gen. Strange's force to kill an Indian belongs to Joe Butlin of Calgary, a sergeant in Steele's Scouts and not to Major Steele as reported in last week's Bulletin. The circumstances are: On May 26 Major Steele, Sgt. Butlin and three other scouts or police with John Whitford as guide left the column on a scouting expedition to the north east and making a big detour came back towards Pitt from the northeasterly direction. As they were scouting away after dark, three to five miles from the fort four Indians, one in a police uniform who was on foot saluted Butlin with "'Tesquai"—wait. This gave the game away and Butlin dropped this man before he had any time to make any further remarks. A somewhat lively time ensued during which Major Steele got a couple of bullets through his sleeves and a second Indian caught a bullet with his back as he was turning to go. His body was found the next day about two hundred yards from where the skirmish took place. The rest of the Indians got away. The first Indian killed was named Ma-ma-nook of Saddle Lake and was well known to many people here. He was a tall man and had policeman Cowan's rifle and tunic on so that possibly he was the man who killed Cowan.

William B. Cameron.
As a young trader for the Hudson's Bay Company he survived the Frog Lake Massacre and wrote of his experience in his memoir, Blood Red the Sun.

William Cameron, the clerk at the Hudson's Bay Store at Frog Lake, had miraculously escaped the massacre at Frog Lake on the morning of April 2, 1885. Using a blanket he was able to blend in with a group of Indian women, eluding the rampaging warriors. Somehow he escaped their wrath that day, endured several months of captivity and eventually told his story in a book. He described in detail the Indian, Meminook, whom McClelland had shot and killed in the dark:

> "When in the early spring of '84, on my way down the Saskatchewan with a trading outfit I first happened across Meminook, he was I thought one of the finest types of the pure Indian I had ever seen. It was at Victoria. He lived at Saddle Lake, thirty-five miles to the east, and I was going his way. The trail was new to me, and when he volunteered to keep me company I was more than pleased. He had the figure of a senator of ancient Rome—tall, graceful, commanding; strong intellectual features; a nose with a classic bend; a voice deep, sonorous and musical. Stretched in the beguiling glow of our camp fire late into the night, he told of war

parties, of Blackfeet scalps won in battle, of camps raided and horses run off. When he arrived with [*some*] the Saddle Lake band in Big Bear's camp shortly after the massacre, Meminook at once looked me up, saying, "While I am in the camp, Kahpaypamachakwayo, (Wandering Spirit), if he loves his life, will be careful how he looks at you."[16]

Cameron went on to relate the last time he saw Meminook and it's obvious from these comments the warrior had an ominous premonition of his pending demise. Meminook was facing his future with a sense of rationalization as he bid the young trader goodbye:

> "The night we camped in the coulee (Stand-off Coulee valley floor) I saw Meminook, his face smeared with vermillion and yellow ochre, leave his lodge buckling on his cartridge belt. I asked where he was going, the reason for the paint.
>
> 'To the fort,' he stood looking down at me with his friendly, engaging smile his fine eyes dancing, he took my hand and pressed it. 'If I do not come back—well, what of it? It is what comes to us all some time. Remember always, Meminook was your friend!' He sprang to the saddle of the restless black stallion—the same Henry Quinn had ridden at Pitt. I did not see Meminook again."[17]

Meminook, Maymenook, Maminook, or Marmaduke (the spelling differs depending on the source but the name means "Hunter") was a "headman"(high ranking council member) from the Saddle Lake Reserve, who lived a few hundred metres north of today's highway intersection. According to local folklore, he held an undeniable belief his people were not being treated fairly ever since the signing of the treaty. He shouldered that responsibility as best he could, desperately trying to improve their lot on the reserve in any way possible. When the rebellion erupted he and several other warriors from Saddle Lake Reserve left their families and rode east to join Big Bear's resistance. Meminook was an extraordinarily tall man. Joseph Hicks, a member of Hatton's Scouts claimed his dead body measured six feet, four and a half inches. Jingo Strange observed his body on two occasions and commented, "Next morning, on passing the spot where he fell, I was struck by the tall athletic figure of the dusky warrior as he lay, like a bronze statue overthrown by some iconoclastic hand."

What happened next certainly gives one a feeling of disgust; however, the facts speak for themselves. Ed Hayes, a member of Steele's Scouts, years later recalled the atrocity:

> "One of the boys scalped Meminook. This scalp hung
> for a long time in a billiard hall which was on the corner
> of First Street east and Ninth Avenue (Calgary). It was
> run by Billy Keohan and George Seabury. Mickey
> McFarlan took a medal, I took a shawl."[18]

A supply wagon driver who hailed from "south of the border" tied a long rope around Meminook's neck, and spurring his horse, dragged the body in wide swinging circles around the flat grassy area where he had been killed. When he tired of this "sport" he cut the rope off, leaving the noose portion still wrapped around the corpse's neck. Another man cut off one ear and carried it around in his breast pocket, displaying it to the morbidly inquisitive. Their justification for these despicable acts was, "When opportunity offers, pay the redskin in his own coin!" referring to the Indian practice of scalping their foe, and also to the atrocities delivered to the bodies of Constable Cowan at Fort Pitt, and the priests and the others at Frog Lake.

There are discrepancies between accounts of the midnight gunfight incident. Meminook was wearing David Cowan's tunic and cartridge belt, although he was not his killer. (Louison Mongrain of the Woods Cree was convicted in Battleford of killing the policeman and later reprieved by the courts.) There is some uncertainty over who shot Meminook for certain, as is the location of where the skirmish occurred. Cameron described it as the Pipestone Creek but distances described by Steele are inappropriate to this location. Cameron is the only person who described the location as Pipestone Creek, yet he wasn't present during the incident. The location may well have been the Old Man Creek, closer to Frenchman Butte hamlet. Many years ago a human skull was uncovered in this area, whereas nothing of significance has come to light at the Pipestone Creek location. Distances described by most of the reports support the Old Man Creek location as being more logical. There is also controversy over who shot Meminook; General Strange indicated Butlin, as did the Calgary newspaper. Steele confirmed Tom McClelland fired at the native. Steele couldn't fire for fear of hitting McClelland on his left, between Meminook and himself.

On the morning of May 27, Steele led his column eastward on the trail the Indians had followed just a few hours previously. The scouts hadn't gone more than a few kilometres when they came across a recently abandoned camp. Steele paused long enough to count 187 campfires, indicating the main group of Indians could not be far away.

Steele detailed scout John Whitford to take five men and explore in advance of the main column of scouts. Whitford, a Métis from Lac St. Anne, was a highly respected, competent buffalo hunter with exceptional skill and leadership abilities. On numerous occasions he had been elected hunt captain and had never failed in producing a successful hunt. He was well acquainted with the country around Fort Pitt, and Sam, confident in Whitford's capabilities, had instantly accepted him into the scouts when he applied at Edmonton.

The six scouts followed the trail eastward and silently moved into some dense bush where Whitford, in the lead, heard a horse stamp its foot. Sitting silently on his mount he listened intently, and a moment later heard an Indian say in Cree, "Wait … wait! Let them come a little further." Steele and the column were approaching in the open, vulnerable to attack and not far away.

Whitford, screened by the bush resorted to a ruse, asking in Cree, "Shall we fight or fall back?"

The reply in a low tone was, "Let us draw them; to fight is no good. We were not sent here for that!"

Whitford turned his horse in an instant and dashed past his men, shouting at them to ride for their lives. The Indians, realizing it was not one of their own who had posed the question, leapt to the pursuit of the scouts. A wild chase ensued with the scouts, leaning low over their racing horses, whipping them hard in desperation. Whitford's ears were filled with Cree war whoops close behind. His issue, broad-brimmed cowboy hat blew off and there was no stopping to retrieve it!

Steele spotted the frantic chase with the endangered men riding hard toward them and whooping, screaming Indians close on their heels. He instantly shouted an order for his scouts to dismount, and for a few to charge ahead with drawn rifles to cover Whitford's "retreat." The column quickly spread out, lying their horses down in a traditional cavalry manoeuvre, ready to repulse the charging Indians once Whitford's men were out of the line of fire. The Indians, seeing the main column, pulled up and turned away, retreating to where they'd come from without testing the accuracy of the scouts' Winchesters. Whitford made his report to Steele, who saw the cowboy's risky antics worth a hell of a good laugh seeing as no one had come to harm. (There's no record indicating whether Whitford got his hat back.)

With the excitement dying down the scouts took a rest break, and just as they were about to remount again, General Strange leading the Winnipeg Light Infantry with the nine-pound cannon appeared, marching up the trail from the fort. The 65th Mount Royal Rifles, under command of Colonel Hughes, were on board the scows, floating down the river from Fort Pitt. Strange knew they were now close to the Indians' main force and he intended to attack them at the first opportunity, hopefully freeing the prisoners. When he reached Steele's still recovering scouts, Strange immediately reacted and formed the supply carrying wagons into a defensive circle as a sanctuary in case they might be forced to retreat. The armed drivers were detailed to guard them while the rest of the column advanced on foot. Should their progress be satisfactory the wagons would then catch up to the column later.

The column marched eastward about eight kilometres, turning up a heavily wooded ravine running from the river valley. The scouts reported that Indians were just ahead and within moments the soldiers could see them on horseback at the top of a long, high ridge on which the Carlton cart trail ascended obliquely to the southeast. This was the militia's first sighting of hostile Indians. Steele described the spectacle in his memoirs: "They were galloping in a circle to warn their camp, their excellent horsemanship and wild appearance making a remarkable picture silhouetted against the blue sky. The ridge had changed since I last saw it in 1876, from a bare prairie to fairly thick woods." This comment indicates the effect the massive buffalo herds had on the vegetation of the prairies. The combination of buffalo hooves cultivating the ground and prairie fires was instrumental in keeping the northern forest at bay. It took only a very short time for the trees to encroach and spread across the northern grasslands as we see them today.

Inspector Perry and the trained gun team were frustrated but still obeyed Middleton's orders to wait in Battleford; therefore, Jingo Strange was forced to rely on a back-up cannon team. Fortuitously, his son Harry was a trained artillery officer who took over command of the cannon and hurriedly instructed four WLI volunteers of the loading and firing procedures required. Harry ordered shrapnel shells to be loaded and determined the range at approximately "fifteen hundred yards." He touched off the cannon and a couple of seconds later the shell exploded in the air above the ridge. A second shell was quickly sent on its way, and as a result there was no longer anyone to be seen on the ridge. The Indians had had their first experience with a cannon they called, "the gun that speaks twice."

Strange ordered his force be extended: Steele's Scouts on the left, the Winnipeg Light Infantry in the centre, and Hatton's Scouts to the right. The trumpeter sounded "Advance" and the force began moving forward in "skirmish order." R. G. MacBeth of the WLI related the event later:

> "We halted momentarily for breath and Major Steele rode up to me with a warning to keep to cover or 'If you don't they'll pot you for sure!' while at the same time he seemed to forget about his own colossal figure seated on a horse seventeen hands high. Once more the bugle sounded 'Charge' and a final assault was made up and over the crest of the ridge. There wasn't an Indian in sight!"[19]

The extended scouts worked their way eastward through the bush on foot, carefully moving from tree to tree. It was slow deliberate progress in the tension-filled air, and several times scouts uselessly exchanged shots with the evasive Indians as the advance continued.

General Strange, the cannon, and wagons were forced to use the main Carlton cart trail as they followed up behind the skirmish line. Towards dark the column stopped a short distance west from the geographic prominence of Frenchman Butte. Strange ordered the supply wagons, which had caught up to the force in the meantime, to form another defensive corral. The armed men put out their bedrolls on the outside of the wagons, with sentries patrolling just outside the perimeter. MacBeth never did understand why the Indians didn't attack at night during the next few days. He was convinced had they done so, they could have made short work of the force. In making these comments he was likely unaware that Steele, fearing this very possibility, had spread his scouts out to provide warning if the Indians began preparing for an attack. Scout Arthur Patton from Edmonton silently slipped through the poplar trees until he was close enough to the Indian camp to observe the campfire's flicker. He kept vigil from this dangerous and vulnerable position until the first hints of dawn streaked the eastern sky. Just as the camp began to awaken he slunk away, backtracking to report an "uneventful" night to Steele.

In the meantime, Colonel Hughes and the 65th Mount Royal Rifles were floating downstream, trying to parallel Strange's advance. On hearing the cannon commence firing on the ridge, Hughes immediately ordered his scows to shore. Leaving their uneaten suppers to grow cold, the battalion disembarked and force-marched to join up with Strange. The departure was so hurried they didn't even bring the barest of essentials, other than their rifles and ammunition. When darkness enveloped them there were no blankets, or even coats, for warmth and only a meagre share of hard tack biscuits scrounged from the generous WLI. There was nothing they could do but shiver through till dawn, without fires or hot tea, trying to catch a bit of sleep. Once again the night was inky black, and oddly, reasonably warm for a change. The surrounding trees a few metres away seemed to hem in the nervous soldiers who knew the Indians "were just out there." Fortuitously, they were left undisturbed during the night.

With the arrival of dawn the force began to advance again with Steele and his scouts on point and on foot pushing their way through the dense trees. On the west side of Frenchman Butte the force came across the Indian's Sundance lodge. Most of the scouts, including Steele,

"First Encounter Ridge." Looking East,
North of the hamlet of Frenchman Butte, the militia had its first
view of the Cree warriors, riding around excitedly on the crest.
This is where the militia first used its cannon, and the
"gun that speaks twice" forced the Cree to flee.

were familiar with the structure and its ceremonial significance. Captain Ernest J. Chambers of the 65th Mount Royal Rifles, never having seen one, described the now barren structure that was before the curious group of soldiers:

> "With a sort of superstitious unease we gazed at the large Sun Dance lodge, stripped of its cover of hides, which the Indians had no doubt taken with them. It was about forty or fifty feet in diameter, and built of solid poplar tree trunks. The cone-shaped roof rested on a row of strong posts about twenty feet high, and all the pieces were tied together with rawhide thongs. At the peak of the roof hung an enormous ball made of cedar (willow?) boughs from which hung, for decoration, a large number of multicoloured cloth streamers. Other similar drapings hung from all the rafters, which gave a gaudy look to the structure. Inside,

about two metres from the entrance, there was a sort of hedge. The space between the wall and this hedge formed a sort of antechamber for the use of the squaws who were not permitted to take a closer look at the mysteries of the Sun Dance. It was evident the lodge had been abandoned in haste and the tracks of the Indians lead [sic] north."[20]

General Strange estimated the opposition to be about seven hundred Indians of which only half would be combative warriors. His own force of men was smaller in number but had the advantage of their cannon, which provided them with superiority on the field. They again advanced with the scouts leading in skirmish order, northward about two kilometres to a coulee that ran east and west. This was a tributary of the Little Red Deer River, which flowed east two kilometres to its main stream that in turn entered the North Saskatchewan River. Strange sensed this as an ideal location for the Indians to make a stand, a reality he would shortly discover.

Frenchman Butte Prominence, Looking East.
Indian Sundance lodge was located just this side of the hill.
The battle occurred about one-and-one-half kilometres north
(to the left) at "Stand- Off Coulee."

The Pipestone Creek crossing, where the "midnight firefight" occurred and in which Meminook was killed, now lies on private land. Access with permission is by travelling east from Fort Pitt on Saskatchewan secondary road #797, then across the creek to a power line and road allowance. Turning southward, a dirt road leads to the bottom of the river valley about two kilometres. The crossing is located to the west approximately two kilometres across a flat hayfield. At the creek crossing, the original Carlton/Pitt cart trail is still visible, as is the trail Steele took in the dark down the hill on the west side.

Many historical books written on the North-West Rebellion erroneously indicate the first deployment of the cannon was made against the Indians on the summit of Frenchman Butte. This incident actually occurred along a ridge about three kilometres north of the Frenchman Butte hamlet where a north-south rural road parallels its base. The cannon was brought into action from the edge of a ravine on the west side of the road, near a farmstead. The interesting fact about Frenchman Butte is—nothing at all happened there in 1885!

The prominence acquired its name from a French fur trader and his Indian wife who had camped in the area in the 1700s. A roving band of Indians killed them both and took their fur bundles to Fort Vermilion for trade. The fort's factor recognized the style of tying the fur bundles and concluded his trader was probably dead and the men in front of him were responsible for the deed. After the Indians left the fort he went out to the butte and found the two bodies.

At the northwest base of the butte the trail forked after it passed around the hill's south side (coming from today's town of Paradise Hill). In 1885 a traveller's choice was to bear left toward Fort Pitt and Onion Lake, or continue north on the Green Lake trail, which leads down through "Stand Off Coulee," the battle site.

The Carlton trail is the subject of a large map accompanied by a twice life-sized oxen and Red River cart at the entrance to the village of Paradise Hill. The local residents have identified the location of the trail through the district with small, white and black signs to designate where the old trail intersected the modern roads as it winds its way toward Fort Pitt.

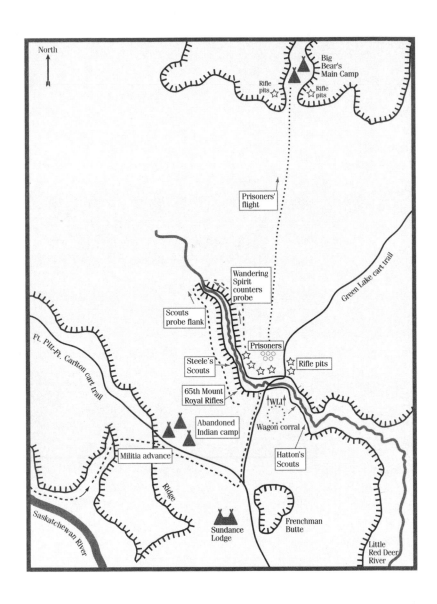

North

Big Bear's Main Camp

Rifle pits

Rifle pits

Prisoners' flight

Wandering Spirit counters probe

Green Lake cart trail

Scouts probe flank

Ft. Pitt–Ft. Carlton cart trail

Prisoners

Rifle pits

Steele's Scouts

65th Mount Royal Rifles

WLI

Abandoned Indian camp

Wagon corral

Militia advance

Hatton's Scouts

Ridge

Sundance Lodge

Frenchman Butte

Saskatchewan River

Little Red Deer River

Chapter 6

THE BATTLE OF FRENCHMAN BUTTE

The Alberta Field Force reached the edge of the ravine now known as "Stand-off Coulee" just as a thick, milky fog was lifting around six thirty on the morning of May 28, 1885. The sun streamed through the last shreds of mist as it melted away from the trees and out of the valley in front of them. Alongside the trail, just at the brink, was a smouldering Indian campfire in which Steele pointed out a half-cooked doughcake (bannock) lying in the ashes. They were very close!

With his field glasses Sam peered through the remnant wisps of mist across the 500-metre-wide valley. It was heavily covered with young poplar trees, alders, and rosebushes on their side, and at the bottom a meandering stream, now in flood, flowed sluggishly through stands of willow. In contrast, the slope on the opposite side was open with the sparse trees giving way to prairie grass that basked in the sunshine. A month earlier prairie crocus blossoms would have flourished across its breadth in the warmth of early spring, giving a blue tint to the grassy hillside. Above the crest to his right he could see strips of coloured cloth hanging in the tree branches, and beneath these banners there appeared to be concealed fortifications. Sweeping the binoculars along the brink of the valley he could make out some rifle pits dug into the ground, carefully camouflaged with grass, tree trunks, and rocks. The cart trail ran from his feet straight down the hill, crossed the creek, then curved downstream for about a half kilometre and abruptly turned northward following a drainage out of sight just under the flags.

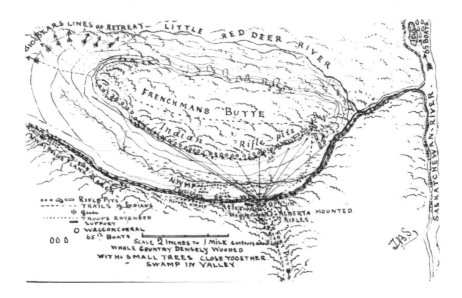

Battle of Frenchman Butte Map.

General T.B. Strange's map of the militia's and Indians' positions at "Stand-Off Coulee." This document was part of Strange's official report to General Middleton at the conclusion of hostilities. The rivers are drawn skewed in relation to the combatants' positions.

Steele and his scouts—at the head of the column—were dispersed along both sides of the trail on which Strange, the wagons, and the cannon were following. Sergeant William Parker, accompanied by a volunteer scout Alex Rowland from Edmonton, were ordered ahead to check out the valley and begin descending the steep trail to the bottom. Nervously glancing across the valley and the surrounding trees Rowland nodded his head slightly toward its crest above and warned Parker in a low tone, "Its an ambush. The Indians are there, I'm sure." The two casually turned their horses and returned to the top of the hill and reported this to Steele.

Sam, in the meantime, kept his scouts out of sight in the trees while Jingo, wanting to see for himself, took another Edmonton scout, Arthur Patton, down the sloping trail to the creek. Both men expected a barrage of rifle fire at any moment but only the song of birds met their ears in the still morning air. The two riders reached the creek where the Indians had torn out a corduroy crossing. Patton attempted to cross first but his horse

The Battle of Frenchman Butte.
Captain Rutherford's sketch, made several days later, depicts the cannon team firing on the Indian positions across the coulee. The original artwork is done in colour with pertinent notations that indicate this location has changed little since 1885. Rutherford must have stood where the monument stands today.

sank instantly to its belly. General Strange was slightly behind and reined his mount in, avoiding a similar fate. Patton's horse lunged and thrashed its way free of the oozing morass and managed to gain dry ground again next to where Strange waited. "There's no point trying to go through here! We'll have to find another place to cross," Patton warned from the back of his mud-splattered, snorting mount. The two returned up the steep track to the nervously waiting force without being fired upon.

Strange had a short conference with Steele, and they agreed the Indians were surely waiting, entrenched with guns ready, on the opposite crest of the valley. Strange drew in a breath and announced to Steele, "Well, we'll find out!" He ordered his son Harry to bring up the cannon. The gun crew rolled it into position in the only open spot available on the edge of the valley, just to the right of the cart trail, and began preparing the piece for firing. Harry determined the range to be "six hundred yards." The cannon was loaded with a pre-measured sack of gunpowder, then the shell; the gunner elevated the barrel and aimed it.

The priming powder and fuse were then set into an orifice at the barrel's base, and at the officer's command, the piece was fired. A deafening boom echoed and re-echoed across the valley as the shell flew toward its target.

The shell went high, whizzing well over the Indian fortifications, exploding far to the north in the bush. Theresa Gowanlock, a captive of the Indians, thought it was "music to [her] ears," despite the fact they had to walk away from their military salvation. The Indians' hostages had earlier been ordered by Big Bear—wisely—to leave the area and walk through the fog abreast of each other so as not to leave a distinct trail. Lacking provisions and extra clothing, they trekked northward toward the band's main camp located in another ravine about six kilometres away. The gun team reloaded the cannon and the second shell also went high as they tried to find the range. Missehew, a warrior in the trenches, later claimed the third shot from the cannon hit the poplar trees about halfway to the tops, just above their heads. Instantly, a fusillade of Indian rifle fire broke out in response from within a few hundred metres of their fortifications.

Steele and his men left their horses under guard just back from the brink of the hillside and took a few moments to pick up extra ammunition and to check their Winchesters. This was finally the big fight they'd anticipated since leaving Calgary and they were going to make the most of it. The scouts dispersed along the ridge to the west of the trail, firing back at the Indians as they advanced in skirmish order downhill to the bottom of the valley.

Strange meanwhile ordered the 65th Mount Royal Rifles to extend and advance down the steep brush-covered embankment below the cannon on the east edge of the trail. The Winnipeg Light Infantry were positioned to the Quebecers' right, and Hatton's Scouts were extended on the extreme right (east) flank where the valley was deepest. The 65th Mount Royal Rifles and the WLI advanced "at the double," with the officers leading them in a military "line abreast" formation. The WLI's scarlet uniforms, along with Steele's red police tunic were a severe disadvantage. Unlike the dark greenish-black of the 65th Mount Royal Rifles' uniforms and the scouts' buckskin jackets, the bright colours "drew fire" as the battle continued at long range. Steele ignored the handicap of being conspicuous, seemingly appearing everywhere exuding confidence and offering encouragement and advice to his men. He continually urged his scouts to

Constable Donald McRae, NWMP.
Although wounded in the thigh during
the battle of Frenchman Butte, he was
not carried out of the valley until after
convincing Sam Steele to allow him to
fire off his last rounds of ammunition
first. Here he is seen after his promotion
to sergeant, and with his Northwest
Rebellion medal. The clasp on the ribbon
indicates he fought under fire.

keep to cover despite bullets slapping into trees beside him. He seemed invincible and without fear as he moved about the firing line.

One of the Plains Cree warriors, Oskatask, excitedly taunted the troops across the valley by jumping up, waving his arms, and gesturing. He called across to the troops, "Tan-et-ese, tan-et-ese!"—his version of the militia command of "Stand At Ease," which he'd previously heard at the forts. He had perceptively noticed that at this command the men relaxed, appearing to lose their discipline; he thought perhaps this might well work here. Moments later he paid the price for being conspicuous by taking a bullet in the wrist while he was waving a blanket at the troops.

Steele led his men downhill, firing sporadically as they went, eventually reaching the bottom of the ravine where the poplar trees gave way to willow that grew in the soft swampy soil. The scouts attempted to push on across it toward the grassy rise ahead. Several were able to cross the swamp bottom to the very edge of concealment while others found the ground ahead of them impossible to traverse even by crawling. It was obvious that continuing the advance would have been foolhardy because across the creek there was no protection on the grassy slope leading up to the Indian positions. They had to be content with lying at the edge of the willow clumps, firing uphill at any movement or puff of rifle smoke they saw. Constable Donald McRae attempted to move from one willow clump to another

Cannon's Firing Position, 1999.
Little change has occurred since 1885.

and slumped to the ground with a bullet through his left thigh. Constable Alexander Dyre crawled over to him and examined his wound; Steele, too was beside him in an instant. Seeing the bullet had passed right through, they helped McRae temporarily bandage the leg with a strip of cloth to help stop the bleeding. Steele ordered the men to carry him out of harm's way, back to where Surgeon Paré could properly treat the wound, but McRae would have none of it and arduously pleaded with Sam to let him at least fire off his last few cartridges at "those dammed redskins." Reluctantly, Sam agreed, and the constable did just that before being carried back up the hill to the doctor.

In the meantime, Harry Strange switched the cannon ammunition to shrapnel shells and these burst in the air over the trenches, sending steel balls contained inside the shell in all directions. These loads didn't seem to have much effect other than to cut off the tree branches above the Indian positions, so he returned to the original delayed fuse explosive shells. These particular shells would explode about one second after they hit, throwing up a geyser of dirt and twigs.

Steele momentarily returned to Strange, advised him of his limited progress, and watched the cannon team involuntarily duck their heads as a rifle bullet ricocheted off the cannon barrel. Strange, relying on his

India battle experience, shouted an order to Harry, "Get those men on the ground! Do the reloading on your knees!" Another slug slapped into the dirt near the cannon's wheel and a musket ball, at its extreme range, fluffed lazily into the grass just to the left of it.

"Someone across the valley has a Sharp's long range buffalo rifle and knows how to shoot!" Steele concluded. The marksman was probably an Indian-sympathizing Métis, Weekwaypan (Trousers), who had become an expert marksman through years of shooting buffalo at long range and would again become very effective against the scouts at Makwa (now Loon) Lake narrows five days later.

The cannon succeeded in wounding six warriors, one of the Frog Lake Massacre participants, Kahweechetwaymot, mortally. He was apparently hit in the abdomen by shrapnel and suffered agonizingly until he died early the next morning. General Middleton's troops later located the grave and exhumed the body to ascertain it didn't contain one of the hostages. The general described the body as, " ... partially clothed and had an eerie look about it, owing to both cheeks being painted red." There may well have been others wounded but these weren't mentioned or accounted for because of their minor status.

Strange ordered Steele to withdraw his men quietly, keeping out of sight, and to bring them back up to the top of the coulee. To mask this move the 65th were ordered to spread out even further and take the place of the vacating scouts. The scouts retrieved their horses and made their way along the valley to the west, cautiously watching the opposite side where Indians occasionally showed themselves, momentarily taking ineffective shots at them. It seemed to Steele their battle line extended indefinitely around the bend of the coulee and to the northwest for over three kilometres! About this time Strange ordered the cannon to be relocated, moving it more to the west so it could support the scouts' movement and fire upon the Indian trenches farther north on the ravine's edge.

Steele was foiled at being able to find a way around the Indians' flank. In fact, Wandering Spirit easily spotted Steele's force working up the valley, and with a few warriors, deceivingly parallelled the scouts. Wandering Spirit was Big Bear's War Chief and Steele had arrested him years before in the Cyprus Hills. Wandering Spirit and his followers had assaulted a party of Cree buffalo hunters and their families near

Wandering Spirit, Cree War Chief.
Steele had had past dealings with Wandering Spirit and regarded him as "a foul, bitter man who could not be trusted at the best of times." The stress from his responsibilities turned his hair white during the rebellion. He was ultimately convicted of murder and executed at Fort Battleford.

Two Riflemen of 90th Winnipeg Light Infantry. *These two soldiers saw action during the rebellion. The soldier on the right is identified as Robert Allen.*

Fort Walsh, maliciously destroying the hunters' teepees, cutting up harnesses, and stealing the horses. It fell to Steele to locate them and bring them to task for their acts, which he eventually succeeded in doing. Steele knew Wandering Spirit to be a bitter foul-tempered man who certainly could not be trusted at the best of times, and now they were again adversaries.

At one point Sergeant Parker volunteered to climb a very tall pine tree to see if he could look across into the Indian positions. Steele agreed to the idea and up Parker went, despite the danger of being seen and subsequently "picked off." From this vantage point he could look over into the rear of their positions. He saw many of the Indians vacating the trenches and filtering northward away from the battle. He reported this to Steele, indicating the Indian's loss of heart in the confrontation. Sam ordered him back on the ground, and with two other scouts, he was then sent to reconnoitre a possible crossing place. Parker's party was able to find a location that appeared to be acceptable and he reported back to Steele. The scouts then returned to the main force, and Steele—

in turn—reported to Strange in detail. In the meantime the cannon was still maintaining a steady slow rate of fire on the Indians' rifle pits, economizing on the available ammunition.

A conference of the commanders was called, and Strange proposed a concentrated attack from the left flank that Steele's group had just scouted out. The drier open area that would have to be crossed was much smaller and provided less risk to the assaulting troops. He believed an attack from that direction would force the Indians into retreating eastward toward the main branch of the Little Red Deer River. Strange expected Middleton and his force would then confront them again in a pincer movement if they marched from the paddlewheel steamboats steaming toward them upriver from Battleford. Middleton only had to be intercepted by a messenger apprising him of the situation so he could land his troops and attack. The plan didn't meet with much enthusiasm from the other commanders, with the exception of Steele. There was also an unconfirmed report that Indians were now firing at the wagons and horses that were corralled at the rear in a small opening of the bush. Strange, fearful of "committing Custer" by being surrounded, and with only one day's rations left for his force and limited cannon and small arms ammunition, concluded a withdrawal was the safest course of action. He reluctantly ordered the commanders to systematically pull their men back.

At the last moment Strange learned Private Le Mai of the 65th still lay seriously wounded and abandoned at the bottom of the coulee. Le Mai's commanding officer refused to recover the private, believing he would die of his wounds very soon anyway. The officer concluded he'd been shot at quite enough for one day. Strange seethed with rage at the man's unacceptable attitude, but rather than take the officer to task for leaving Le Mai, he set an example by personally heading up a stretcher party. With Father Prevost, Doctor Paré, and two stretcher-bearers, Jingo went back down to the firing line to retrieve the soldier. Under intense hostile rifle fire, and with Strange's urging, Prevost quickly administered an abbreviated "last rights" amongst the flying bullets. Strange ultimately manned one end of the stretcher, when one of the bearers faltered, and they struggled up the hillside to safety. The wounded man later made a surprisingly quick recovery; in just a few weeks he was up and gingerly walking around at Fort Battleford prior to the force's departure home to Montreal.

***Paddlewheeler Steamboats* Marquis *and* Northwest.**
The Marquis *has run aground on a sandbar and is pushing itself off. These boats were used extensively for troop and supply movement during the rebellion. Their success over a period of about fifteen years on the North Saskatchewan was mainly due to their captains' river skills—a lost art.*

The last off the field of battle at about 9:30 a.m. was Sam Steele and his scouts as a rear guard to cover the column's retirement. The battle of Frenchman Butte had lasted for only about three hours! The force pulled back about eight kilometres where they bivouacked in a defensive circle for the night. The 65th Mount Royal Rifles continued on, marching back to the river and their scows only to find they had vanished. The flotilla's officer, and the men left with them for security, had slipped downstream for protection behind an island, out of sight. They subsequently found the scows were too cumbersome and awkward to be able to return back upstream. With the river scows' disappearance there was no alternative for the 65th but to make the return march back to Strange's camp. They rested for a couple hours, ate what rations were left, then late in the day Strange led the entire exhausted force back to Fort Pitt and to their welcome tents, hot food, dry clothing, and warm blankets. The last official military battle on Canadian soil was over, but more severe fighting was yet to come and this time it would be Steele's Scouts in the fray, alone.

Frenchman Butte battle site is readily accessible. Signage on Highway #3 northeast of Lloydminster on the east side of the North Saskatchewan River directs the traveller north about ten kilometres to a small federal historical park. The first portion of the road north is paved until a bend where it swings west. At this bend continue north on the gravel road, past the west side of the Frenchman Butte prominence. This impressive mound dominates the entire countryside from every direction, visible for miles.

The small park on the north side is within a few dozen metres of the Indian rifle pits. A descriptive sign and clearly defined pathways lead the visitor to a giant stone with a plaque that graces the valley crest. The signage incorrectly claims the McLeans occupied one of the pits during the battle when in fact they used it during the previous night only. While the battle was in progress they were walking northward to another camp as described. Governmental interest in the battle site is virtually non-existent and many of the pits dug in 1885 have slowly disappeared as they fill with nature's debris of leaves and fallen trees!

On the south side of the ravine, directly across from the stone cairn, is a second and lesser known cairn, marking the militia's positions. From the Indian rifle pits it is just visible in a small opening on the opposite side. Access to this site is by hiking down the slope and up the other side. The cairn is beside a fence that borders a cultivated field. The cannon location during the battle was in the only opening present, and remains almost exactly as was depicted in Captain Rutherford's sketch. He must have stood on the very spot where the cairn now rests to make the sketch. The original trail to the bottom is faintly discernible a few metres west of the cairn's position. Of additional interest is a steel pole near the militia cairn. This pole is one of the few remaining original telegraph poles fabricated in England and shipped to the west for the telegraph line when it was constructed between Battleford and Edmonton in 1882.

Frenchman Butte Indian Rifle Pits Monument (north side).
Looking south. Steele's Scouts were deployed on the right, the 65th Mount royal rifles to the centre-right, the Winnipeg Light Infantry on the centre-left, and Hatton's Scouts/cavalry to the left. The Indian rifle pit, originally dug in 1885, is visible in the foreground. The militia's monument is on the other side of the valley, at a spot just above this monument.

Militia Monument (south side).
Marilyn Brown and local historian Edgar Mapletoff on a cold November day. The background nearly matches Captain Rutherford's sketch made in 1885.

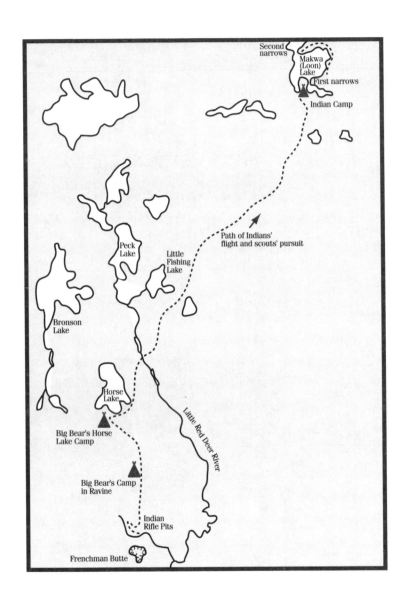

Second
narrows

Makwa
(Loon)
Lake

First narrows

Indian Camp

Path of Indians'
flight and scouts' pursuit

Peck
Lake

Little
Fishing
Lake

Bronson
Lake

Horse
Lake

Little Red Deer River

Big Bear's Horse
Lake Camp

Big Bear's Camp
in Ravine

Indian
Rifle Pits

Frenchman Butte

Chapter 7

TO FREE THE HOSTAGES

At Fort Pitt the entire force finally had a chance to rest for a day, cleaning and mending their equipment and clothing, much of which had been in use every day since they'd marched from Calgary. Nearly every member of the force exhibited patches somewhere on their garb because of the harsh conditions. Rifleman John Florin lamented, "Our clothes are wearing out, we're in tatters," even though his service with the Queen's Own Rifles under General Middleton was not nearly as severe as that seen by the Alberta Field Force, and especially that of the scouts. The chances to have a real bath were few and far between up until now because they'd been constantly on the move since leaving Edmonton, so many of the men were contracting body lice; their spare time was often spent going over their bodies and clothing "picking cooties"! They attempted to combat the problem by swimming in the river and boiling their clothing in salt water, then spreading it out to dry in the sun on some rocks or tall grass. The result of this treatment caused the red uniforms of the Winnipeg Light Infantry to fade into a deep pink hue.

Under Strange's orders Steele detailed two scouts to paddle a canoe down the river and locate the scows of the 65th Mount Royal Rifles that had gone missing. They and the twelve men were ultimately located, tied up to the shore of an island, several kilometres downstream from where the militia had disembarked. The barge crews had discovered the vessels were too cumbersome to pull by shore line back upstream against the river current, so they eventually floated on downstream to Battleford, empty. During the previous few days Strange had sent several messages by scout courier to General Middleton and received no response or direction on continuing operations. In frustration he lamented, "Like the crows sent off from the Ark they never returned!"

Steele had directed several Métis scouts to remain near the battle site and monitor the Indian activity after the force's withdrawal. These scouts were less than enamoured with what they thought was a risky proposition and consequently failed to keep contact with the Indians; ultimately they became disconcertingly uncertain of the Indians' whereabouts. On May 30, the force again marched east from Fort Pitt for about eight kilometres. They camped on a plateau near Old Man Creek, not far from Steele's skirmish in the dark. The weather once again deteriorated to a dreary rain, seeping under the tents and making the men damp and uncomfortable. A vexed Steele sent a second party of scouts back to the battle site area to determine where the Indians had gone. They spotted just a few of them wandering around the rifle pits, apparently retrieving previously abandoned supplies. They also found indications that the main group had moved on further north but how far was questionable. The next day was Sunday, and despite a downpour, church services were once again conducted. This allowed the troops, with the exception of the patrolling scouts, to remain in camp. They spent the day resting in their tents, listening to the rain, playing cards, writing letters or telling stories, and "picking cooties."

On June 1 the entire force, with the scouts leading as usual, marched back to the battle site, circling the ravine to the west where they had to press their way through the young poplar tree growth. It was so dense that the horses could pass only in single file; the supply wagons and equipment were forced to remain at the river camp. They camped about four kilometres north of the ravine in a meadow, and many of the soldiers walked back to view the Indian rifle pits in the evening despite the lingering rain. Everywhere they looked lay the Fort Pitt looting: food, clothing, equipment, wagons, carts, bales of fur—all abandoned. The men that wandered about the battle area were amazed at the extent of the fortifications. Some of the rifle pits were as long as fifteen metres and two and a half metres deep, with rifle loop holes in a log barricaded front. Steele believed there were about three hundred pits in all, able to accommodate over five hundred Indians. One of the scouts that knew Wandering Spirit, Imassees, and a couple of the other warriors they had faced, believed these men had had previous battle experience against the U.S. Cavalry in the States prior to the war with Custer. He felt that such battle knowledge could account for the elaborate defensive trench system along the valley's edge. In fact, in defensive warfare the Cree traditionally used entrenchment and barricades since they first acquired firearms and possibly before then.

Steele had sent his scouts out on patrol as usual when Strange finally received a message from General Middleton advising he would arrive at Fort Pitt by paddlewheel steamboat the next day. Strange assigned Brigade Major Dale, NWMP Sergeant William Parker, and twelve scouts to ride to the fort and escort General Middleton and his militia back to his camp. They left late in the evening and while passing near Frenchman Butte, Sergeant Parker heard faint shouting coming from the direction of the butte itself. They reined in their horses, listened, and shouted back a reply. Out of the trees stumbled three bedraggled men: the vanguard of the captives just released by the Chipewyan Indians. The reticent Chipewyan had finally found a way to separate from Wandering Spirit's Cree nation, and after setting the captives free, had started on their return journey to the Cold Lake Reserve. The group consisted of Reverend and Mrs. Quinney, William Cameron, Henry Halpin, Francois Dufresné, and several other Métis families. As they got near to the scouts Quinney erupted with the built-up stress of the past months and began weeping openly, clutching Parker's saddle stirrup in relief. Major Dale detailed two scouts to guide the group back to Strange's camp, north of the battlefield. They arrived at the camp about eleven at night and were immediately ushered into the general's tent. Strange ordered up the best food his cook could muster. While it was being prepared William Cameron, finally laying in the safety of a militia tent, started to shake and tremble uncontrollably. An anonymous NWMP officer (Steele?), heedless of the force's no liquor policy, came into the tent and stretched out on the ground opposite Cameron and began questioning him about his captivity. He passed a large cup of rum over to him, advising, "Drink it. It'll help calm you down." With all the excitement it was very late before any of the ex-captives were able to sleep. This rescue left only one more group of white captives to be recovered: the McLeans, Mrs. Gowanlock, and Mrs. Delaney.

Strange immediately called Steele into his command. "Steele, those people that just came in are fortunate the Indians let them go. From what they tell me there appears to be a breakdown in the Indians' leadership. I don't think Big Bear has control anymore and Lord knows what will happen to the McLeans and the rest of the hostages. It's imperative we free them as soon as possible, so I want you to take a 'flying column' and go after them as hard as you can. There is great risk for you in this order because of the limited manpower available but I can promise you that reinforcements will follow up as quickly as possible." Strange also indicated the freed captives heard a steamboat whistle just before being found by the scouts so Middleton would certainly arrive by morning.

Steele was acutely aware his opportunity to go after the Indians would vanish with the arrival of Middleton. He left Strange's tent and went stomping through the scouts' camp to wake them, roaring, "Get up men! Get up! Get eight days of half-rations and all the ammunition you can and follow me."

The camp erupted in bedlam as the scouts scrambled to get things together, grab some supplies, saddle up, and get ready to ride. A total of 21 NWMP, 22 Alberta Mounted Rifles, and 21 volunteer scouts answered Steele's call. Just as they were about to ride out, one of Strange's staff officers marched up with an order for Major Hatton to remain behind. Hatton was shocked, and utterly dumbfounded! The chance to be part of the most important action of the campaign was snatched away from him at the last second. Steele later remembered seeing Hatton's frustration: With tears welling up in his eyes, he bitterly struck his saddle horn with a riding crop. The hit was so violent that the crop shattered; but an order was an order and he did remain behind!

R.G. MacBeth, a soldier in the Winnipeg Light Infantry, was awakened by the commotion and was thrilled at the sight of Steele's column riding out by twos at a full gallop. He later wrote, "I remember how these fellows—magnificent riders, every one of them—wheeled out on the gallop, and followed where the tracks showed most of the Indians had gone."[21]

The Indians' tracks that the scouts had discovered earlier indicated they had filtered away from the rifle pits to the north, and their separate

Louison Mongrain.
Mongrain assumed the role of
Chief after the murder of Chief
Seekaskotch (Cut Arm). He
was also instrumental in the
protection of Mrs. Delaney,
Mrs. Gowanlock, and the
McLean family, which
provided the grounds for
court leniency in the shooting
of Constable David Cowan at
Fort Pitt.

trails eventually came back together as they entered a gorge eight kilometres due north of the battlefield. Steele and the column gingerly entered the ravine, following the creek bottom until it opened into a wide valley where the Indians had camped. Steele looked up at the sides of the ravine and several scouts probed the crest. A perfect place for another ambush, he thought. Then one of his scouts shouted down to him, "The whole hill up here is covered with rifle pits!" In fact the Indians had prepared to ambush the pursuing force if it followed them after the battle. On the floor of the valley were dead campfires, more abandoned carts, supplies, fur, and equipment strewn about, but not an Indian.

Time was wasting and the column was pushing hard on the trail, onwards. It led out of the valley north and westward. They found a note tied by a strip of cloth to a tree branch. On a page torn from the book *Robinson Crusoe*, W.J. McLean, the captive chief trader of Fort Pitt, had written the following:

LOOK FOR US UP THE HILL
FROM HERE
N.W. FROM HERE
W.J. McLEAN & FAMILY
ALL WELL 27TH MAY 1885
MAY GOD PROTECT US

The next Indian camp Steele encountered was in a parklike setting of pine trees on the south end of Horse (now Sidney) Lake. The Indians and their captives had spent the better part of two days at this camp, recuperating from their flight through the bush after the battle.

Along the entire trail, Steele's column encountered barricades of fallen trees, "and everything the Indians could possibly do to impede their progress accomplished, except to stand and fight." In the rush of their departure neither Steele nor any of the scouts had thought to bring even an axe and this lack of foresight hampered them considerably. The trail led past the east side of Horse Lake and north along the west side of the Little Red Deer River drainage system. It crossed soft, horse-tiring, swampy ground, through muskeg and thick forest. Steele marvelled at the endurance of the Indians: hundreds of them, women, men and children, young and old. How had they covered this most difficult terrain on foot, dragging their possessions along in wagons, carts, and travois? He wondered in amazement. His scouts had had great difficulty while carrying only the barest of necessities on good horses.

W.J. McLean, an experienced employee of the Hudson's Bay Company, had been transferred to Fort Pitt in 1884. He found the nearby native communities "restless and turbulent." Using the influence of "the Company" and his reputation for fairness (Indians referred to him as "Straight Tongue"), he was able to calm the atmosphere to some extent, but this only lasted over the winter, and in April unrest resumed at Frog Lake. During the siege of Fort Pitt he was able to negotiate an arrangement for the NWMP to depart by river scow on the condition that he and his family became semi-volunteer captives and that he swear an oath to Wandering Spirit not to attempt escape. By doing so he undoubtedly saved the lives of virtually everyone in the fort. Had Wandering Spirit and Imassees attempted it, they and the other Cree warriors could have easily overrun the fort's inadequate defences.

Little Red Deer River Ford.
Captives and natives alike faced water up to their armpits at this ford on their flight north from Horse (Sidney) Lake to Loon Lake.

McLean described the ordeal the Indians and captives went through as they fled northeast from the Alberta Field Force:

> "Owing to a false alarm the camp at Horse Lake was broken up in confusion at the break of day on the first of June, and in a heavy rain we travelled all day through swamps and woods in a northerly direction to Loon Lake. That night we camped drenching wet and had to lie down to rest in that condition (having no change of clothes) which was not congenial to good health or feelings. Before sunrise we were ordered to be up and march again, and as we emerged from our tent into the cool air and continued drizzling rain we were for a moment obscured by an aqueous haze arising from our bodies.
>
> The heavy rain had swollen the many creeks we met to overflowing their banks, all of which we had to wade through, to a depth often up to our waists. We camped that night, both wet and weary, and on the following day about noon we reached the ford at Loon Lake."[22]

It was almost noon, and the men and horses were in need of a rest, when the scout column came upon a small meadow somewhere just south of Little Fishing Lake, which Steele estimated to be about 50 kilometres north of the camp where Strange's militia remained. The column dismounted to munch on a couple of hardtack biscuits while the horses grazed on the poor quality meadow grass. Just before re-mounting Canon McKay and a Calgary volunteer scout, Thomas "Jumbo" Fisk, rode out across a meadow ahead of the column—and into trouble. Years later McKay related the story:

> "I spied some Indians armed with rifles. The trail would lead them (toward the meadow) within fifteen yards of my position, so I determined that they should not pass a certain point on the trail. I watched with my rifle at my shoulder and ready to pull the trigger. When the leader reached that point I fired and dropped the Indian to the ground. He had been merely grazed on the head and in a moment he was up and moving fast. A few shots were fired over his head to see if he could increase his speed."[23]

When McKay fired, "Jumbo" Fisk was just a few yards behind. At the sound of the gunshot he put the spurs to his horse and instinctively charged the Indians. One of them fired at Fisk and he yelped in pain as the Indian's bullet struck, severing his little finger and shattering his elbow, as well as knocking him off his horse.

Steele and the rest of the scouts instantly reacted and charged across the meadow at the treeline on foot. Several more shots were exchanged before the Indians melted into the trees, away from the scouts' onslaught. Steele later described their hunt through the trees for the warriors:

> "When I was about 50 yards in the woods I heard behind me a fierce war whoop and turned, expecting to see an Indian, but it was our friend, Canon McKay, who, like the majority of western men and boys brought up among Indians, could utter a war whoop which would make Sitting Bull turn green with envy! His eyes

Red River Cart.
*These carts were constructed entirely from wood and "shaginappi"
(dried buffalo hide) and pulled by a single oxen or pony. Famous for
their capabilities and easy repair, their deliberately ungreased wheels
could be heard squealing a far distance across the prairies. Canada's
military still uses a modernized version as a transport trailer. Shown
is an authentic reproduction located at Fort Walsh.*

were blazing as he hurried along uttering his fierce yells. He was dressed in a pea jacket, felt hat and moccasins, his pantaloons were tied with strings around the ankles, and he was obviously full of fight."

The column skirmished through the trees, chasing the fleeing Indian warriors, and was eventually ordered to reform. McKay scoffed at why there wasn't a dead native on the ground. "Of course, I could have killed the Indian, but after all I am a clergyman and I did not plan on killing an Indian if I could frighten him into doing my bidding."

The Indians were now using an old Red River cart trail that went north from Horse Lake, crossed the Little Red Deer River (called Monnery today) on the south end of Moonshine Lakes, and then veered east across a swampy bay of Little Fishing Lake before resuming a northerly route. The going was exceedingly difficult for the pursuing scouts and one of the horses went down in the swamp with a badly broken leg. The scout, realizing the end of the chase had come for his part, levered a shell into his rifle and mercifully put a bullet into his horse's head. He silently uncinched the saddle, hefted it and the saddlebags over his shoulder, then dejectedly began walking back down the trail to "Pitt." Eventually *26 men* were sprinkled along that trail, all walking back toward the fort with their equipment over their shoulders!

Around midnight Steele finally called a halt about ten kilometres to the northeast of Little Fishing Lake. They dismounted and in the dark built a makeshift protective barricade on a sharp "hog's back" ridge between two sloughs, using their saddles, deadfall, and rocks. As soon as daylight seeped over the eastern horizon a short four hours later, the column was saddling up and moving again. Breakfast in the saddle was gnawing on a hardtack biscuit. The trail continued northeast through thick alder, poplar, and occasionally an open stand of pine. They passed two campsites where the fleeing Indians had spent the nights. At each of the sites the scouts found abandoned or broken equipment that the Indians left behind to lighten their loads. Eventually the trail turned more northerly, passing along the west side of Goose Lake and on to Makwa Lake (now Loon Lake) narrows.

When the scouts came to the top of a long ridge, they dismounted and lay down, looking at the scene below them. Steele noted it was 10:00 a.m., June 3, 1885:

> "Before us lay a large and very beautiful lake with many pretty bays; a long point jutted out from the east side of it, and might be an island; it was densely wooded to the water's edge. Along the west shore a dry swamp of spruce and tamarack extended, and a semicircular range of hills, bounding a small prairie below us, came around to where we lay."

Steele's Scouts were at Makwa Lake and below them were the Cree and the captives.

With my 25-year knowledge of the old but still usable trails and by following the participants' memoirs, I have retraced the route taken by Big Bear and Steele from Frenchman Butte to Steele Narrows on Loon Lake. None of the Indian or militia campsites are officially identified and are difficult to locate without expert guidance. The Cree camp north of Frenchman Butte can be accessed by vehicle with permission of the landowner. It's located about eight kilometres north of the battle site, to the east of the same north-south gravel road that leads you to Frenchman Butte rifle pits. Follow a road allowance east through the trees for about two kilometres towards the valley with a gate through the fence on the right. From this gate a trail leads to a picturesque valley where the Cree camp was located. Today you'll find a water-filled dugout and a cut-line that climbs a rise to the south. The rifle pits are located on each side of the line; however, they are not as prominent as those of the Frenchman Butte site and require diligent probing to locate.

Big Bear's camp at Horse Lake (now shown on maps as Sidney Lake) is not marked. The gravel road continues from the camp mentioned above in a northerly direction to a "T" intersection. Turn left and travel west about five kilometres, go through a gate and along a grazing lease access trail, which turns north to pass the small, narrow, Long Lake. About two kilometres north of the lake, at a fork in the trail, is an oil company sign. East of this intersection is the campsite chosen by Big Bear's band to rest for two days before journeying on. The trail leading northeast used by the Indians and Steele's Scouts is only navigable by all-terrain vehicles. In many places "The Rebellion Trail" is not easily discernible, but it becomes more defined again east of Little Fishing Lake where it's known locally as "Theret's trail." Used now as a recreational snow machine and all-terrain vehicle trail, it winds to the north and east, and about halfway to Loon Lake it becomes very difficult to trace. The location of the scout, militia, and Indian camps along this stretch are unknown.

In researching this part of the campaign, like Steele, I am in awe at the stamina of the fleeing Cree. Men, women, and children, dragging along a few possessions and a meagre supply of food, were able to traverse this exceedingly difficult terrain in only three days, camping just twice on the trail. They were indeed "tough"!

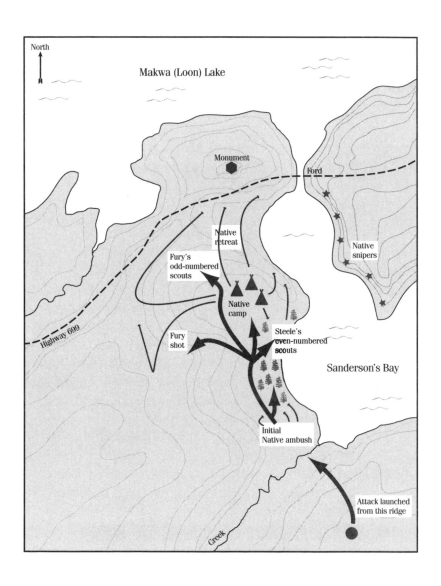

North

Makwa (Loon) Lake

Monument

Ford

Native
retreat

Native
snipers

Fury's
odd-numbered
scouts

Native
camp

Highway 699

Fury
shot

Steele's
even-numbered
scouts

Sanderson's Bay

Initial
Native ambush

Attack launched
from this ridge

Creek

Chapter 8

CONFRONTATION AT LOON LAKE

Steele halted the column near a huge, flat rock, just back from the brink of the hill overlooking Makwa (now Loon) Lake. He and Sergeant Joe Butlin moved closer to the brink and looked down on the panorama below. A bay of the lake (now called "Sandersons Bay") extended from below their position northward to a narrows, and then expanded out into the main body of water that stretched to the far shore several kilometres in the distance. The hills to the west formed the side of a basin in which nestled a small Indian camp, snuggled against its north end. To the right, or east, of the camp was a spruce and tamarack swamp that separated the meadow from the shoreline of the lake. Through his binoculars Steele could clearly see the teepees, along with several carts and derelict wagons, sprinkled across its grassy floor. A few Indians were ambling about, one intently tending a campfire with a tea pail strung over it. In the distance to the north, another party of Indians was visible, wading carefully across the shallow narrows onto what he thought was a large island.

Steele and Butlin, having seen enough, slipped back from their vantage point and returned to where the men waited with the horses. Steele stood on the large rock and began to outline the order of battle to his men. First he asked the men to "number off," then he gave his orders in a clear steady voice: "When we get near the camp I'm going to have Canon McKay demand their surrender. Should that fail, you even-numbered men will follow me into the camp and free the prisoners if they're still there. Sergeant Fury will lead the odd-numbered men through the camp, then spread out and move up the hill. I want this group to keep it clear of any Indians so they don't fire down on us. We want to push them out of the village, north toward the ford, forcing them to cross. That way we can identify the captives as they wade across to the other side." The scouts checked their 45-75 calibre Winchesters and the issued ammunition, making certain they were prepared. Leaving their horses behind, they began moving downhill on foot toward the teepees below.

At the base of the hill a lazy creek trickled toward the lake through a sprinkling of spruce and tamarack growing along its banks. As they moved closer to its banks several Indians ineffectively opened fire on them from the trees on the other side, signalling a warning to the camp.

Steele, realizing a parlay was now out of the question, sprang ahead with a revolver in each hand, shouting, "Come on men, kill all the Black Elk you can!" and led their rush across the creekbed. The scouts, shouting and whooping as they ran, initially held their fire as they charged. This forced the Indians to break from their cover and flee back toward their camp through the trees. They continued their rush northward across the meadow, pushing the retreating warriors through the treed swamp ahead of them, thus protecting the scouts' right flank.

Steele and his men reached the camp and flushed several Indians out of the teepees. Some ran for the swamp and others toward the surrounding hillside, a couple of warriors being wounded as they fled. The Indian rifle fire coming from the protective swamp was hot and heavy; bullets seemed to zip through the air everywhere, kicking up clumps of dirt as they struck the ground around the charging scouts.

Fury and his men fanned out and returned fire as they moved past the teepees toward the base of the ridge as planned. Fury could see Indians moving along the ridge line above him in a southward direction, a move that would eventually surround the scouts if it succeeded. Steele also recognized this possibility and shouted an order for Fury to lead some of his men up the east-facing slope to prevent it. Fury's group spread out and kept climbing quickly from bush to bush and rock to rock, firing as they went. The speed with which they fought up the hill succeeded in forcing the warriors to retreat back to the north again. Meanwhile, scout Fielders on the far, eastern end of the charging scouts flushed out an Indian right in front of him only three metres away. He instinctively pulled the trigger of his Winchester, killing him instantly. Today a marker indicates the spot where the native warrior died.

Across the bay, Indian warriors who had crossed the narrows earlier that morning, rushed back to the aid of their comrades fighting the scouts on the other side. They opened fire from along the shoreline on the opposite side of the bay but many of their antiquated rifles' shots only caused minor wounds when they struck their targets. Being fired at low velocity, their nearly spent bullets and—sometimes—round pebbles barely penetrated the buckskin jackets of the scouts.

Just as Fury, Coryell, and McDonell reached the summit, they came into view of a Métis, and Indian-sympathizer, Weekwaypan. He coolly had the sights of his long-range Sharps buffalo rifle trained on the hillside, and when its front bead fell on Fury's chest he deftly squeezed the trigger. Fury spun and fell from the impact, rolling and sliding down the steep slope, a slug through his chest on the right side. Canon McKay was the first to reach the wounded Mountie. He jerked open his jacket, stuffed a handkerchief onto the wound, and temporarily propped up Fury—now gasping—on the hill's steep slope. The charging, yelling scouts carried on past the two, over the hill and along the ridge, clearing the Indians off the vantage point. They had been nearly surrounded—like Custer—and it was only Steele's and Fury's aggressive leadership that carried them through their peril.

In the meantime, Steele and the even-numbered men, went through the camp, taking a couple of wounded Indian prisoners, and setting fire to the teepees, destroying supplies and equipment. They saved two wagons and several axes that they needed later for the return trek to Fort Pitt. By this point in the battle a half hour had passed since the initial charge commenced from the top of the hill.

The Indians themselves were in three groups: the warriors from the camp were driven into the lakeside swamp, or to the second group on the ridge who were pushed off its crest by the scouts' uphill charge, and the third group of warriors could only snipe at the scouts long range across the bay from the east side.

Despite rifle fire coming at them from across the water, Steele and his men continued through the swamp and along the shoreline, forcing the warriors northward toward the ford. They returned fire whenever they could; one of the scouts killed another Indian on the opposite bank. One scout was momentarily standing behind a tree, with his shoulders visible on each side, when a bullet smacked into the opposite side—dead centre, but not through. Weekwaypan ejected another empty cartridge from his Sharps. Hicks later lamented in his account of the events, "We had to respect the man with the Sharps rifle." With all the fast shooting some of the scouts had trouble holding their Winchesters because the barrels began overheating. They now had the retreating Indians caught in a pincer between the two scout groups, thus forcing them across an opening that was about 45 metres wide. With scouts firing on both sides, the Indians crossing the opening were caught in a gauntlet of bullets! Three Indians—Komenakos, Mestahekpinpiko, and Pwacemocees—were killed, and several others were wounded trying to run across the meadow.

Steele later gave a detailed account of his part in the confrontation:

> "They [Indians] posted themselves under the shelter of the hills opposite to us and again opened fire, their bullets tearing the bark off the trees round my trumpeter, Chabot, and myself. Chabot offered me his rifle to fire at the red men, who seemed to be making fine practice, but I told him to go ahead as I had something else to do, and a few minutes later I heard an Indian Chief [Wandering Spirit] leading his men with yells of encouragement around the hills to my left front, and to meet the attack sent by the men [Fury's group] on my left up the hill."

Wandering Spirit was shouting to his warriors to attack the scouts. He seemed to be everywhere, urging them on to fight back. Many of the warriors were low on ammunition and reduced to firing stones out of their old muzzle-loading rifles—a deciding factor in the battle. One of the young white captives, Kitty McLean, was braving the scouts' fusillade, wading across the ford for the second time with her eighteen-month-old brother John in her arms, when a bullet ripped between her face and little John's head and another put a hole in her fluttering shawl. *The scouts were firing at everything that moved!* One of the Indian warriors was killed in the water near her, his body eventually floating to shore where another white marker stands today. As the bullets zipped past Kitty she involuntarily ducked her head, revealing her hair and face. One of the scouts, seeing her more clearly shouted out, "My God! There are white prisoners there. Stop the shooting!" They stopped firing on those crossing the narrows for awhile.

The shooting eventually settled down to a slower but steady pace, with scouts on one side of the hill (where the monument now stands) and Indians on the other, only metres apart and neither daring to peer over the brink. Both sides shouted insults back and forth, and scout Hicks remembered hearing one of the boys asking the Indians how they liked killing helpless women and children. The reply was to the effect that the scouts should "Go to Indian Hell!" The scouts could also hear moaning coming from Indians along the opposite slope, indicating that some were lying there, seriously wounded.

Steele asked Canon McKay to call to the Indians in Cree to surrender. At great personal risk he attempted the task three times, but each time without success, being driven down by whistling bullets. Some of the natives listened momentarily, but one in particular kept on shooting, forcing the two into changing positions each time the preacher shouted to them. Steele assessed the sniper: "He was an exceptional shot and armed with a good rifle." Perhaps it was Weekwaypan.

Across the water some time later W.J. McLean waved a piece of cloth and tried to acquire a cease-fire at the bidding of some of the frightened Indians. One of the warriors had ridden to Chief Cut Arm's teepee at a second camp and persuaded McLean to come to the narrows to stop the shooting. McLean, like McKay on the opposite side, tried several times to get a cease-fire. This proved fruitless as he too became a target of the scouts; his Indian captors, who feared for his safety, finally pulled him down.

While the battle was raging Chief Seekaskootch ("Cut Arm," an amputee) of the more reticent Woods Cree from Onion Lake Reserve, was attempting—like Big Bear had done at Frog Lake—to keep his men from becoming involved in the fighting. He had proclaimed, "I will shoot any Indian who shoots a whiteman!" and returned inside his teepee located east along the trail, away from the fighting on the east side of the ford. Upon re-emerging he was shot in the back of the head. Osawan and Mamikinow were also murdered at the same time in the confusion.

The chief's young son, Missehew, later related to listeners the story of what followed:

> "I ran across a dead Indian and when we checked he had been shot with a small bore rifle. We went on and found another wounded man. He told us it wasn't soldiers that got them.
>
> "They [the scouts] are good shots." he said. "My brother took his leggings and put them on a stick, lifted them up. Immediately there was three shots and three bullet holes in the legging. One of the three was a left hander with a hooked nose. After he shot he would get up and turn around slowly before disappearing. My brother took careful aim at this man and shot him."

There is some speculation that Missehew's brother shot scout William West.

Records indicate Chief Cut Arm's murderer was Little Poplar, a radical Plains Cree who Duncan McLean later described in a magazine article: "He wore a Stetson hat, adorned with plumes, and in his broad leather belt carried a Bowie knife and two six-shooters. He was not of a friendly disposition. He had nine wives, all his sisters whom he married successively as each reached womanhood."

Along with Big Bear's oldest son Imassees and several other Indians, he escaped to the United States. After the battle they split from the main group and travelled southeast through some valleys west of Barthel, away from the expected militia pursuit sure to follow. These warriors remained in exile and were never taken to task for their involvement in the rebellion or for the murder of Cut Arm and the others.[24]

The fighting died down; most of the Indians had melted into the bush or had crossed the ford at the narrows to relative safety. Steele found his men down to about fifteen rounds of ammunition each and still there were no indications of the reinforcements that General Strange had promised would follow them up. The only choice left was to fall back, so he reluctantly detailed a small rear guard party of six men under command of an NCO to remain and cover their withdrawal. On several occasions they opened fire on a few Indians at the narrows, and in all probability fired at W.J. McLean as he tried to communicate with them. (Investigation indicates this rear guard built a fire beside the big rock on the hill top, heated up bullybeef cans and ate the contents as they monitored the Indian activity from this vantage point.)

With a final glance at Loon Lake and the narrows sparkling blue under billowy white clouds, Steele turned and followed his column. As they made their way southward and down the winding trail he was still hopeful of meeting the promised reinforcements from General Strange. With new supplies he fully intended to return, cross the narrows, and try again to free the captives who he believed—correctly—were in great peril.

Sam Steele, now mounted up, his red tunic fairly glowing in the sunshine, waited at the top of the hill until every man was past. The scouts collected the redoubtable little Irishman Sergeant Fury and three wounded Indian prisoners, loaded them onto wagons, and pulled them down the trail about five kilometres where they stopped for a short rest. Scout William West had taken a musket ball through the knee into his thigh, and after being bandaged re-mounted his horse with the rest of the scouts. He had no intention of riding home in a wagon!

Scout Joseph Hicks later claimed that of the 47 men who made the assault at Loon Lake, seven were wounded bad enough to require some medical attention and nineteen in total were hit. Official records stated that five Indians died but there's no record of the number of wounded. Hicks also stated that Loneman, a wounded prisoner they captured in the camp, claimed years later there were 75 or possibly 100 Indians wounded in total at Frenchman Butte and Loon Lake narrows. Steele, in his report to General Strange claimed his own group killed five Indians and Fury's accounted for seven, to make a total of twelve. In addition, there were the three Indians who were murdered. This tally hardly matches the official records, which seem to misrepresent this violent battle and downplay it as a minor incident in the campaign.

Steele sent General Strange a message that included a brief report of the action with Canon McKay, Sergeant Butlin, and scouts Gisborne and Fielders. General Middleton had arrived at Fort Pitt; he and Strange were in bed when the scouts came in to report at about 2:00 a.m. Strange pleaded with Middleton to immediately send the mounted reinforcements he had promised Steele, and the irritated jealous Middleton replied, "Not a man! Not a man! Who is this Major Steele?"

Steele's Scouts at Loon Lake Narrows.
Sketch by Captain Rutherford looking north during the final withdrawal
on June, 10, 1885. Steele's attack was launched from this hill on the
Indian camp located beyond the scouts, just above the lead scout's head.
The narrows (now called Steele Narrows) is on the right side of sketch.

Same Location as Seen Today.
Marilyn Brown at "the big rock" where Steele commenced his attack at
Loon Lake. Looking north the narrows are about where Marilyn's head is.
This is almost the same view as Captain Rutherford's sketch above.
(Note that this site is not a designated historical park.)

He stomped back into his tent to contemplate how some upstart major—worse yet, an NWMP officer—could cast a shadow on "his campaign."

Despite his serious wounds, Fury seemed relatively jovial and determined not to let his obvious pain affect the progress of the column. The retiring and exhausted group travelled about 22 kilometres before calling a halt for the night. The return trek was, thankfully, considerably easier than when they came initially. With the aid of the axes obtained from the Indians' camp the scouts were able to clear many of the obstacles that had hampered their initial pursuit to Loon Lake. The column finally met up with Middleton's belated advance on June 6. His force had been in camp, diligently making pack saddles and travois for their supplies and equipment that were to replace the wagons for the anticipated difficult trail ahead. Middleton had abandoned his marching militia, of which rifleman Florin was a member, in favour of using only his mounted cavalry. Florin deploringly commented in his diary, "We [Queen's Own Rifles] are left behind—great indignation prevails."

Middleton chose two Gatling guns rather than any heavy cannon in consideration of the difficult terrain the scouts reported his force would face. The Gatling gun was a crude predecessor of the machine gun, fired by turning a meat-grinder crank, which rotated a series of rifle barrels. As each barrel came into alignment a cartridge was driven into the barrel; the gun discharged and then extracted its empty round. The rate of fire was about a hundred rounds per minute or one shot in a little less than a second. Because of the unwieldy nature of the gun it wasn't particularly accurate and had to be mounted on a carriage (just as a cannon is) to facilitate movement, but its advantage was its considerably lighter weight. Middleton felt the gun was of little value other than to give moral support to his command, a lesson learned at the siege of Batoche. He exclaimed, "Though the Gatlings had been well and pluckily worked, they had proved unsuitable for the kind of fighting we were engaged in—the physical and moral effect on our enemy had been very slight."

The next morning, the general himself finally appeared, riding regally along at the head of his column. Steele with his military savvy had his scouts lined up in proper formation to the side of the trail. He advanced at the appropriate moment and greeted the general. Steele saluted and gave a full, formal, verbal report of what had occurred over

The Gatling Gun

the past several days, including a summary of his battle at the narrows. At Steele's conclusion, Middleton curtly dismissed him with an order to carry on and overtake General Strange who was marching past Frog Lake to the Beaver River Crossing store. The expectation was that Big Bear's band would travel there following a large circuitous route. He correctly believed they had to replenish their supplies and ammunition soon and this was obviously the most logical place to accomplish this need.

Steele was immensely disappointed with Middleton's orders and sought out the general's aide-de-camp, Captain Frere. Sam pleaded the need to remain and act as escort because of their knowledge of the terrain ahead, while secretly hoping for another chance at freeing the hostages. Captain Frere willingly presented Steele's case to the general who finally recognized the policeman's value and relented, allowing those scouts who didn't require medical attention and had rideable horses to remain and guide his advance back to Loon Lake.

General Frederick Middleton.
Commander of all the forces that suppressed the North-West Rebellion.

Lewis Redman Ord, a member of the survey scouts attached to General Middleton's force, later wrote anonymously in a printed article about the feelings of the moment:

> "The astonishment on every face and the curses, not loud but deep heaped on the general's head could be understood and appreciated only by those present and, indeed, had I not actually been there I could hardly believe that a man calling himself a soldier could dawdle and delay in such a ridiculous senseless manner. When one remembers that he had some two hundred men in his command and that forty miles distant along a cart trail, Major Steele with forty-six men had the previous morning attacked probably thrice that number of Indians, driving them out of their camp, and was at

General Middleton's Pioneer Clearing Trail. *Captain Rutherford's sketch of June 1885 shows Captain Dennis and his men. The trail from Frenchman Butte to Loon Lake had to be cleared to allow the Gatling gun and column through. The whole distance was covered with dense young poplars that still flourish today. In places this trail still exists!*

that moment, waiting for us; that each horseman could carry from three to five day's provisions and reach the scene that night; that supplies and forage could be rapidly pushed along the trail after us; and that had even half the horses been killed by the journey, their loss would have been nothing compared with the value of a decisive blow, and the Indians were so demoralized by Steele's attack."[25]

Ord, clearly very impressed with Steele, goes on to say:

"A few miles on we found Steele and his command— that officer not having been able to follow up his advantage from lack of supplies and ammunition and

Taking the Gatling Gun Through the Moose Hills. *Captain Rutherford's sketch indicates the difficulties encountered on Big Bear's trail. The box on the forward set of wheels is a caisson, carrying ammunition and spare parts for the gun (on the bottom set of wheels).*

at once notice the genius and forethought required to make a force march with due regard for proprieties. What a vast advantage education confers on a man; here is Steele, a poor ignorant devil of a Canadian, with his seventy men away up in this blasted, howling wilderness, you know, and no wagons, no tents, no comforts; positively nothing, you know. We come upon a little open patch and see drawn up and waiting for us Major Steele's troop of mounted men, bronzed by sun and wind and toughened by hardship and exposure. Led by a *MAN* and unencumbered by red tape, they pushed rapidly after these Indians, fought and beaten them and, after waiting vainly for support for two days, were now ready to show us the way. Truly they are

Steele's Scouts Ford the Narrows.
This photo, taken in June 1885, is just a few metres north of today's Highway #699. The monument is located behind the horsemen, on top of the hill.

Fording the Second Narrows.
Steele's Scouts, leading General Middleton's cavalry, followed the trail of Big Bear's band around the east shore of Loon Lake to the north side. Here they found a second narrows and muskeg obstacles which caused Middleton's decision to halt the pursuit. This photo, taken by Captain Peters looks south across the lake toward Steele Narrows.

like the scouts one used to read about, yet beyond some lines barely mentioning the fight, I have seen nothing written of this plucky officer and his command."[26]

In contrast, Middleton had difficulties with the pursuit, lamenting how "the weather was very hot, [and] the mosquitoes and 'Bulldogs' [probably horse flies] were terrible; however we all bore it with Christian fortitude, and the occasional big 'D' excepted!"[27]

Middleton's force arrived at the narrows on the evening of June 7 and bivouacked back from the south hill that looked northward on the demolished Cree camp and the narrows. The next morning the force crossed to the opposite side where they discovered several new graves. He ordered them opened to ascertain they contained none of the captives' bodies but found only the dead warriors. A little farther on the scouts came across a dead Indian woman on her knees with a rawhide thong around her neck, slumping away from a small poplar tree. She was an invalid who was unable to keep up with the rest of the band in the harsh country of the north, to which they were fleeing. Sits-By-The-Door, deeply fearing the soldiers, had chosen suicide as the alternative.

The force followed the fleeing Indians' trail around the east side of Loon Lake in a circuitous route, eventually coming to a second narrows on the far north side. At this point the general ordered the Gatling guns and crews to bivouac while the remainder of the force struggled on and established a camp on the west side for the nights of June 8 and 9. Just beyond this camp they encountered another series of defensive rifle pits, recently excavated by the Cree as the trail wound through willows and across a muskeg that Middleton declared "impassable" despite Steele's confidence in being able to continue. The general's inept riding, miring his horse in the swamp, undoubtedly influenced this decision as he personally examined the terrain. The force had ground to a halt, to the end of its "epic" advance. On the morning of June 10 they began retracing their steps, back around the lake, re-crossing the narrows and down the trail to Fort Pitt.

As usual, Steele and his scouts acted as a rear guard for the main column during the withdrawal. Middleton, in true British military fashion, moved his force with an extremely conservative nature. He was not about to be caught "sleeping." Scouts were in the front, cavalry followed, and of course, Steele and his contingent were the rear guard—just in case.

Captain Rutherford seized an opportunity and remained at the rear, sketch pad in hand. As the scouts dejectedly made their way up toward him his pencil recorded the moment almost as well as a photograph would have. This sketch was made looking north from where the scouts initially commenced their attack on the teepees, visible in the background behind the leading scout's head and clearly identifiable in the original artwork. In the far background, to the upper right, is the narrows where the Indians as well as hostages forded the shallows, then continued along the hillside and out of the sketch to the right.

Middleton indicates that on June 11, after two fatiguing days on the return trail, the column arrived back at Fort Pitt without incident.

Steele Narrows is located on secondary Highway #699, ten kilometres west of the town of Loon Lake. On the north side of the road, at the pinnacle of a steep hill, is an interpretative cairn with descriptive plaques dedicated to the battle at Loon Lake. Sprinkled around the area are white cement markers designating where some of the Indians were killed during the battle. Looking directly south, one marker is visible on a ridge about a kilometre away. This is where Scout Fielders killed an unidentified Indian at very close range. In the valley just beyond this ridge out of sight from the cairn's vantage point is the location of the Indian campsite that the scouts attacked. The spruce and tamarack swamp is virtually unchanged in over a hundred years; however, dense bush has infringed on the entire area, making this feature inaccessible in summer other than by boat due to a lack of trails through the dense bush and deadfall.

Chief Seekaskootch was killed over a kilometre away from the east side of the narrows, nowhere near the location of the fighting. The Mistahay Musqua Native Treatment Centre now resides close to this campsite. From where the highway crosses the narrows, the view to the north across the lake is virtually identical to sketches of the time and remains as Steele described it, "a large and very beautiful lake with many pretty bays!"

Chapter 9

NORTH TO COLD LAKE

General Frederick Middleton's military entourage, including a bitterly disappointed Sam Steele and his scouts, trundled back down the trail to Fort Pitt. Middleton had no intention of following the Indians despite being so close, and it was beyond Steele how he planned to free the white captives. It seemed the task had been left up to Strange and his fractured Alberta Field Force who were now camped at Beaver Crossing south of Cold Lake. After arriving back at Fort Pitt, Steele had a lengthy talk with some of the released captives about the past two months, hoping to glean some tidbits of information that would enable him to confirm the Indians' destination. Each accounted for the events from opposite perspectives but they agreed it was fortunate more bloodshed had not occurred, with only providence intervening to prevent it from happening.

Middleton finally came to the conclusion it was necessary for his force to march for the Beaver River store, which was located about 25 kilometres south of Cold Lake, to support General Strange. The Alberta Field Force had hacked, crawled, and staggered through the nearly impassable country from Fort Pitt, past Frog Lake, and northward in a dash to cut off the Indians. The advance scouts of the force arrived at the outpost only minutes before the first Indians, foiling their intention of raiding the store for the desperately needed food and ammunition. From the store the force took two whole days to hack and corduroy their way to Long Bay on Cold Lake, near the present location of the provincial park. Middleton brought Steele's Scouts along with his column

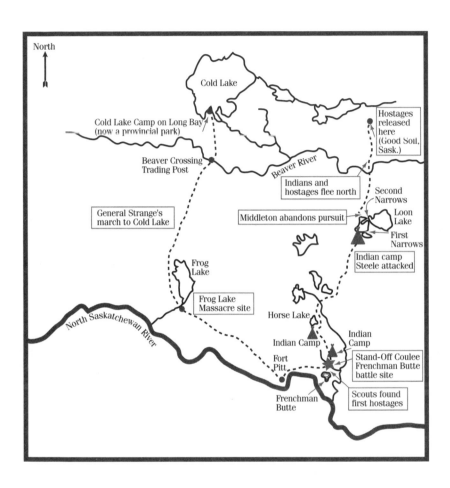

North

Cold Lake

Cold Lake Camp on Long Bay
(now a provincial park)

Hostages
released
here
(Good Soil,
Sask.)

Beaver Crossing
Trading Post

Beaver River

Indians and
hostages flee north

Second
Narrows

Loon
Lake

Middleton abandons pursuit

General Strange's
march to Cold Lake

First
Narrows

Indian camp
Steele attacked

Frog
Lake

Frog Lake
Massacre site

Horse Lake

North Saskatchewan River

Indian
Camp

Indian Camp

Stand-Off Coulee
Frenchman Butte
battle site

Fort
Pitt

Scouts found
first hostages

Frenchman
Butte

Pulling the Cannon Through a Muskeg.
*This example of artwork depicts members of the 65th Mount Royal
Regiment and the Mounted Police "Gun Crew" struggling through a
musheg on the trail to Cold Lake, somewhere near Frog Lake. The 65th's
drudgery earned them immense respect and the title "The Alligators."*

and arrived on June 14, after a leisurely march in summer-like weather, along the trail previously hewn out by Strange's pioneer brigade.

Steele and his scouts conducted a few meaningless patrols of the area around Cold Lake while the general spent two days on the lake, fishing! A report reached Middleton concerning some additional unsettling discoveries at Frog Lake; he ordered Steele to investigate the report's validity, then continue on to the main camp back at Fort Pitt. Steele, inwardly pleased to be relieved of Middleton's dawdling, led the scouts south and in due course determined the report was false. The task proved uneventful so, as ordered, they continued on to Fort Pitt. The scouts' glory days were over and they languished at the fort for nearly a month.

Life in their camp, located on the hill north of the fort, was simply boring. The food was pitiful; Middleton made sure the best always went to "his militia" who were not allowed to even share their issued rations with anyone else, let alone the scouts. Sam tried every technique in his administrative repertoire to get his men better food, new clothing, and

Middleton and Strange Confer.
*Captain Rutherford's sketch of Middleton and Strange in a conversation
at the Winnipeg Light Infantry's bivouac by Long Bay on Cold Lake. Note
the up-turned cowboy hat, a trademark of the Alberta Field Force.*

General Middleton's Force at Fort Pitt.
*Sunday Church parade at the conclusion of hostilities.
Steam-powered paddlewheel riverboats,* Marquis
(largest) and Northwest *at the landing.*

Mealtime for the Cannon Team.
Captain Rutherford captures one of the team flipping a flapjack in the frying pan while his buddy enjoys his pipe, sitting in the campfire smoke to get away from the mosquitoes.

replacement equipment to no avail. This resulted in widespread pilfering by the scouts, a practice that held some satisfaction in outwitting the general, and of which Steele purposefully remained ignorant. He admitted that on several occasions he undoubtedly ate supper at the expense of the general himself, thoroughly enjoying every morsel, and never questioning for a moment the food's source.

Rifleman Florin of the Queen's Own Rifles also described the situation in his diary, indicating how widespread this problem was within the whole force: "Biscuits will be dealt out, (pilfered earlier) a great deal of dissatisfaction exists between officers and men concerning the distribution of Regimental stores which are not being dealt with proportionally."[28]

Middleton knew what was happening, yet was powerless to control it. He went as far as issuing a futile order that any soldier caught giving away rations would receive a month of hard labour for his generosity. The pilfering was clearly not confined to the scouts or to the Alberta Field Force. By this time most of the scouts were literally living in rags. Although a few had scrounged potato sacks to make shirts, their trousers were often torn to their knees, and boots sported twine lashing to hold

Horse Racing, Fort Pitt Style.
Sketch by Captain Rutherford, July 1885. The scouts participated in wild reckless horse racing to relieve the boredom of languishing in camp for days on end. Cheering militia crowd the sidelines at the finish.

the tops onto the soles. Even Steele's scarlet tunic was no longer immaculate, showing its wear with mended bullet holes in the sleeves, rips, and un-cleanable smudges. They were a sad looking lot!

During the time Steele and the scouts lazed around the growing militia camp they kept themselves occupied with a little fishing in the North Saskatchewan River, playing cards, fighting "cooties," and indulging in horse races. The races were exciting, wild, "free for all" spectacles. As Captain Rutherford sketched, the still weary ponies did their best to dash to the finish line amongst the cheering soldiers lining the edges of the course. For the first time since they'd left home there was mail waiting for many of them. Scouts and militia alike sprawled in the sunshine alongside their tents reading over letters and writing their own home. Edward Lovell of the 90th Winnipeg Light Infantry even mailed one of his hardtack biscuits, embellished with a suitable inscription on its almost impregnable crust, to Elizabeth Bailey as a keepsake. This biscuit now rests in the RCMP Museum in Regina not far from Sam Steele's scarlet tunic!

Big Bear Surrenders, July 2, 1885.
This sketch, which is now known to be inaccurate in detail, is the
Imperial War News' *rendition of Big Bear's surrender to Sergeant W. Smart.*

On June 18, word spread through camp like a prairie fire: The last of the captives were free near today's Goodsoil, and the need for the force and Steele's Scouts was clearly at an end. The steamboats *Northwest, Baroness,* and *Marquis* were already tied at the landing, waiting to load the troops, get up steam, swing into the current, and head downstream and home.

On July 2, Big Bear surrendered to members of the NWMP near Fort Carlton. He simply walked out of the bush with his young son, unannounced, giving himself up to a dumbfounded Sergeant William Smart and three constables who by chance happened along. General Strange claimed Smart was likely the only man in the northwest who had not been looking for Big Bear and that final act in itself held immense irony.

The civilian scouts under Steele left Fort Pitt on July 3 for their return journey back to Calgary via Edmonton. The police section of his scouts were ordered to accompany the militia by steamboat to Battleford then on to Swift Current, and ultimately back to Calgary by CP Rail

Cree Chief Big Bear Awaiting Trial.
Note the variety of dress amongst the NWMP guards.

because of a contract that existed between the government and the Canadian Pacific Railway for troop movement.

Middleton had one more last duty for Steele and his scouts to perform. A report he received indicated looting was occurring on the Saddle Lake Reserve. Teamsters returning to Edmonton had taken it upon themselves to collect anything of value along the way as spoils of war. The reports received indicated wagons were loaded full with farm implements and other loot that the teamsters conveniently "confiscated" from the Indians on the reserve. Steele directed Sergeant Parker to take a party of scouts and quickly ride ahead to put an end to this illegal activity. They made quick time to Saddle Lake and succeeded in intercepting the teamsters, and with some suitable admonishments, returned the items to the rightful owners. The scouts continued homeward past Victoria to Edmonton, making far better time with nearly empty supply wagons and unhampered by the marching militia.

Along the way Sergeant William Parker's marksmanship was challenged by some of the scouts. Parker (a bit of a braggart) had a legitimate reputation for being a superb shot, so when a scout spotted a sharp-tailed grouse in the grass just outside their camp he told Parker it presented the chance to test his real prowess. Parker requested permission of Steele to prove his capabilities by shooting the head off the bird with his service pistol. Steele was also intrigued and laughed at the difficult challenge, saying, "I'll tell you what I will do, Parker. If you shoot it the first shot, I'll give you a gallon of whiskey on arrival in Calgary." The wager was on. Parker cocked the pistol then crawled through the grass to about 30 metres from the bird on the ground, its head held vigilantly

Steele's Scouts Locate the Prisoners.
This sketch depicts the moment the scouts encountered the Indians' prisoners who had been released to find their way back to Fort Pitt.

high.[29] He sighted on it and squeezed the trigger. The grouse never flew again, and the men erupted in a chorus of cheers and guffaws. Steele marched over and asked, "What's going on here?"

"Parker's going to eat chicken for supper, Sir!" chortled a scout's reply. Neither Parker nor Steele divulged in their journals whether the bet was ever collected.

The Steele brothers sadly parted company on Friday, July 10, 1885 never to serve together again. Sam rode away from James's farm at Beaver Lake on into Edmonton where the scouts had bivouacked. They then

Paddlewheeler Steamboat Northwest.
*The Northwest, tied to shore and unloading cargo. This magnificent
paddlewheeler would come to a sad ending shortly after the rebellion just
downstream of Edmonton with a load of post-rebellion celebrants. The
Captain called for "slow ahead" and got "full ahead," putting her up on a
gravel bar and splitting her hull.*

took up the trail southward to Calgary, down the well-worn track carved
by hundreds of supply wagons that had shuttled back and forth over the
summer. Richard and Godfrey returned to their regular policing duties
around Edmonton.

On July 18 Sam Steele, at the head of his proud but rag-tag cowboy
scout column, followed Nose Creek toward the Bow River valley and
Calgary. Mayor George Murdock, out for a leisurely ride, spotted them
coming in the distance just after noon and rode for town as hard as his
horse would run.

"The boys are coming! They'll be here within the hour!" He shouted,
spreading the word as his horse galloped down Stephan Avenue. Calgary
erupted in pandemonium! A welcoming arch was already erected at the
entrance to town, and Mayor Murdock, at the head of the throng
consisting of practically every person in town, welcomed the scouts back

home. He orated an emotional welcoming speech outlining how Steele had engaged the enemy, "often times at great disadvantage, having done so without loss of life to themselves, coming out of the fight with credit and honour."

Sam graciously replied on behalf of his motley and tired contingent. Everyone gave three patriotic cheers for the scouts and the Queen, then the crowd parted, allowing the column to ride on into town.

Several days later the town hosted a huge banquet at the Boynton Hall with about three hundred and fifty guests attending the grand occasion, according to reports in the *Calgary Bulletin*. Steele was presented with a diamond ring and accolades flew like the bullets in their previous battles. Steele rose and eloquently responded, drawing to the gathering's attention he had not volunteered for the duty, rather it was an order, and he in turn credited the men under his command for the success they enjoyed. It was a wild evening, even by Calgary standards, and more than one of the attendees of the function spent some of it in the police cells for "overdoing it!"

Steele's Scouts were paid off and disbanded, each going his own way with his memories of the last great adventure. The scouts, excluding NWMP members, each received up to $2.50 per day plus rations and forage for his horse. If he claimed the loss of a horse a reimbursement of $150 was made by the government. NWMP members only drew their regular pay; their service was deemed to be part of regular duties. It took three years of intensive political pressure for the police members to acquire eligibility for the North West Canada Medal which all other participants in the campaign received shortly after returning home. Veterans of the Frenchman Butte and Loon Lake battles received a clasp that was attached to the medal's ribbon, bearing the word "SASKATCHEWAN" to signify having been under fire.

The six convicted culprits of the Frog Lake Massacre would pay the price for their violence on the gallows at Battleford on a blustery cold November 27, 1885. Their bodies were cut down, thrown in a wagon and transported to burial in a common grave below the fort.[30] Some of the others escaped to the U.S.A. to live in exile, a few never returning to Canada. Many of the Indian bands were to suffer dreadfully repressive restrictions and confinement on their reserves for years to come. Deemed as implements of war, they were forbidden to own a rifle or a horse, or

The Boynton Hall, Calgary.
The hall (centre) was the scene of a boisterous "Welcome Home" banquet and dance, honouring Steele's Scouts.

Executed Indians' Grave, Fort Battleford.
This mass grave is northeast of the fort. Eight Indians, who were convicted of crimes associated to the rebellion, were hanged on November 27, 1885 and unceremoniously interred. They included Wandering Spirit, Round-the-Sky, Bad Arrow, Miserable Man, Iron Body, Little Bear, Crooked Leg, and Man Without Blood. The last two men were executed for killings committed near Fort Battleford.

to leave the reserve without written permission rarely granted under oppressive Indian Department policies. A vengeful, strong-willed government forced them to work for even the most meagre assistance: food, clothing, medical needs, farming equipment, and livestock. No work—no help, was the department's motto for years as it systematically attempted to force an end to the natives' traditional way of life.

The Canadian Pacific Railway was complete, and the flood of homesteaders filled nearly every train heading west. From the train stations they spread across the plains that so recently had been covered with the ebbing and flowing tides of buffalo. Except for the police members, the scouts' guns were hung on pegs, never to be used again in confrontation.

The Canadian West would never be the same! A new, modern world blossomed across the territories, and in twenty short years evolved into provinces as part of the Dominion of Canada.

EPILOGUE

As with many historical books, the reader is often left pondering, "I wonder what became of them as time went by?" Some of the participants in the North-West Rebellion continued on with well-documented lives, others seemed to have slipped into obscurity and just fade away. This chapter gives an overview of the careers of some of the story's central characters.

Samuel Benfield Steele

This undaunted Canadian hero was through only part of his unbelievably distinguished career when the North-West Rebellion occurred. He returned to policing the CPR railhead as it reached its completion. On November 7, 1885, along with a host of other dignitaries from the east, he attended the ceremony for driving the last spike of the railway at Craigellachie, B.C. Examination of a well-known photo of the event oddly doesn't reveal his face among the assembly. It's been suggested that at the very last moment Sam inexplicably stepped back from the group, and out of the historic photograph, despite having every right to be standing beside W.C. Van Horne when Donald Smith (Lord Strathcona) performed the honours.

In 1884 two gold miners in the Kootenays of British Columbia were robbed and subsequently murdered at their claims. The local constable investigated the incident, and in 1887 arrested Kapala, a Kootenay Indian, confining him in jail at Wild Horse Creek to await trial. Word of the arrest reached the band's Chief Isadore, and he reacted by leading a group of warriors to retrieve Kapala from his confinement by force.

Sam Steele Leads D Troop.
Peace had returned to the Kootenays and the job was done. Steele leads his troop back to Alberta in August 1888. (Steele is in white helmet).

The chief used the opportunity to also demand the policeman and the local Justice of the Peace leave the area immediately for the sake of their scalps. The threats were effective; the local settlers were left without protection while the natives, bolstered by their success, began actively intimidating them. Liquor availability became a factor as well when white and Chinese traders—seizing their opportunity—made sure it flowed freely at good profit to them.

In June 1887, Sam received a directive to move a substantial force of police from D Division to Golden, British Columbia and await orders for further deployment. In the meantime negotiations with the Kootenay Chief Isadore were underway with an agreement being reached for Kapala to stand trial and the native band to receive additional lands to enlarge their reserve. Sam's mounted force was about to form up and ride out when they received news their supply boat *The Duchess*, which had already left, had capsized just a few kilometres out of Golden and sank. Most of the supplies were ruined, including the horse feed, uniforms, and officers' personal gear; so, consequently it took the entire day to retrieve whatever was salvageable. Despite this setback the march continued southward.

Steele's orders were to establish a post near the confluence of Wild Horse Creek and the Kootenay River. Within hours of the force's arrival, Steele had men at work laying out the buildings, and construction commenced on Fort Steele under the scrutiny of the curious local Indians. Steele next set out to deal with the native situation and held a parlay with Chief Isadore. Sam acted shrewdly with the chief, giving a little here and little there, but always working toward establishing police authority. He deliberately chose to illustrate the force's authority by using the same constable that the natives had evicted to conduct the official arrest of Kapala. Steele himself acted as the magistrate, a normal practice in those days. He heard the evidence, found it very lacking, and rightfully acquitted the native. Other parlays occurred between Steele and Chief Isadore over the next months, with Sam assuring Isadore that the police were not there to destroy the native people, but to be fair to all so they could live in harmony. Isadore continued to exasperate Sam as he continually changed his mind on his demands. When Sam finally confronted him, admonishing him that he was acting in a shameful and foolish manner and that continuing to act in such a way would ruin his chances of consideration from him or the government, the chief mended his ways. Relations had a marked improvement and construction was started on an industrial school nearby as an act of reconciliation. Sam, by his good judgement, had quelled the disturbance and the Kootenays remained peaceful. Steele and the force rode out of Fort Steele on August 9, 1888, heading east over the Crowsnest Pass. Nine days later they rode through the gates of Fort Macleod. Fort Steele stands in tribute to this day, serving as a major tourist attraction in southeastern British Columbia.

When Sam returned to the Fort Macleod area he met the daughter of a Quebec Member of Parliament, who was visiting as a summer guest of Sam's cohort and friend, Superintendent A.R. Macdonell. After a thoroughly pleasant courtship Marie Lotbiniere-Harwood and Sam were married on January 15, 1890. The couple eventually raised three children: Flora, Gertrude, and Harwood.

On January 29, 1899 Sam received a telegram ordering him to the Yukon to police the gold rush. Typically of Sam he was on the first train to Calgary, and then the train to Vancouver where he got on a boat to Skagway, Yukon. Here he worked closely with the Commissioner of the Yukon, his old troop commander, James Morrow Walsh. Walsh had retired from the force a few years before but accepted the offer of a position as Commissioner of the Yukon Territory that lasted for the duration of the gold rush.

Sam Steele and Marie Lotbiniere-Harwood.
Wedding photo, January 15, 1890.

Sam found Skagway to be the roughest place in the world, where robbery and murder were everyday occurrences. He came face to face with the infamous "Soapy Smith" and his gang of some 150 hoodlums. Soapy was a "Mafia style" underworld governor of the territory, controlling most of the illegal activities so commonplace there.

Steele was directed to upgrade the Chilkoot and White Passes' customs entry points located at each of their respective summits. Among other responsibilities, these posts collected the appropriate customs fees for entry into Canada. The daily duties of the officers were accomplished, despite the harrowing weather and the incredibly demanding living situations.

Sam went down to Bennet Lake where he and Commissioner Walsh gazed spellbound on the *thousands* of expectant prospectors' tents that lined the lakeshore, biding time until spring ice break-up. Each of them intended to float down the lake and through the dangerous Miles canyon of the Yukon River and Sam sensed a disaster looming, with inept men taking on the wild river rapids in inadequate boats. To prevent this, he dictatorially established safety regulations for all boats attempting the river run. This was so successful that over seven thousand boats ran the river with a loss of only five lives, a tribute to his "off-the-cuff" law making.

In the meantime the customs houses on the passes had accumulated nearly $150,000 in fees, and there was a need to transport this cash outside to Victoria. The

Sam Steele's Children, 1901.
Harwood, seated, endures; Flora,
standing, is bored; and
Gertrude offers an impish grin.

problem was Soapy Smith and his gang was sure to waylay the shipment, probably in Alaska, beyond police protection. Using a cleverly devised ruse, Sam had the shipment carried in regulation kit bags by three police members who were leaving the area under pretence of a transfer to other duties. The three carried the money literally under the noses of a suspicious Smith and his gang, to the safety of the bank in Victoria, British Columbia. Shortly after, the infamous Soapy Smith met his end in a shootout with a vigilante group on a dock in Skagway, thus saving Sam the eventuality of confronting him.

Sam's next task was to calm the boom town of Dawson. At Dawson he employed members of the Yukon Field Force to act as guards at the local banks and government buildings that handled all the gold. He also established an undercover detective team (the first in NWMP history) to ferret out information on criminal activities. Violaters were slapped with

Sam Steele, Commander, Lord Strathcona Horse, 1899.
Note the similarity of the uniform to that of the NWMP and Steele's
riding posture—no cowboy slouch!

penalties: both monetary, and with hard labour chopping wood "at the woodpile," a humiliating duty in the eyes of the offender. Steele drove himself hard, working eighteen hours and more a day. As a result the territory slowly began to settle down; the lawlessness subsided and finally he left the Yukon in a tumultuous send-off in late September 1899.

The disheartening force's internal events at the end of his Yukon service eventually led to his resignation after 25 years of faithful service. He was offered a number of positions within the force, but he was denied the one he desired the most—that of Commissioner—despite extensive lobbying by his influential friends.

The Boer War erupted in South Africa that same year and the unemployed Steele jumped at the challenge of leading a cavalry contingent, funded by his friend, Donald Smith. Lord Strathcona Horse, a cavalry regiment (now an armour regiment stationed in Edmonton) acquired the undaunted Sam Steele as its first Commanding Officer! Sam launched into his second military career, leading his battalion

Steele in South Africa.
*Sam Steele (left) in an impromptu conference with Lord Baden-Powell
(facing camera) in Pretoria, South Africa.*

brilliantly. One of its members, Sergeant Richardson, earned the Victoria Cross under Steele's command.

After the Boer War, Steele once again returned to policing, at the request of Lord Baden-Powell (founder of the Boy Scouts), formulating and commanding the South African Constabulary, again patterned after the NWMP. Just as in Canada, they developed a reputation for fairness, and decisiveness in a similar atmosphere to that of Canada, metering out justice to settlers, and natives alike, all across the South African frontier.

Sam's last service to his country was for the third time in the military. He was appointed as a Major General, commanding the 2nd Canadian Division in England during the First World War.

In 1918 Steele finally received the recognition that had been a long time in coming. He marched before the King of England, and received a knighthood. He now held the honourable title of "Sir Samuel Benfield Steele"!

Despite the notoriety and prestige that came with the title, Sam was a saddened man who had in reality been deserted by his own country, where bureaucratic politics prevented him from attaining his desires. In resignation, he began to formulate rudimentary plans to retire in Calgary, and began some preliminary house hunting through a business friend of his back there. This dream never materialized; he seemed to have just given up as he slipped toward his final day on January 30, 1919. Sam's body was returned to Canada, and a "full military honours" burial occurred, in Winnipeg, Manitoba.

Samuel Benfield Steele.
January 5, 1849 - January 30, 1919.

Sam was certainly not without fault, as no man is, but he was a real genuine Canadian hero who dedicated his life to "Maintaining the Right!"

Steele's Funeral Procession, 1919.
Funeral of Lieutenant -General Sir Sam Steele, K.C.B.
Canadian generals acted as pall bearers.

General Thomas Bland Strange

"Jingo" Strange, unlike Steele, didn't march back to Calgary and a triumphant celebration. Instead, he and most of the Alberta Field Force were ferried by steamboat downriver from Fort Pitt to Swift Current. There he said his goodbyes to the militia who continued their way back east by rail. The remnants of the force, which originated from the southern Alberta area, were returned by train for disbandment in Calgary.

Strange, like Steele and many of the others who served, seemed to run into difficulties with Ottawa. Recognition of what he had accomplished was exceedingly slow in coming and even his military pension had been suspended when he took the position as the Alberta Field Force commander. Ottawa became reluctant to re-institute it so he was forced to conduct a bureaucratic battle to have it reinstated. In the end his ranching enterprise—the Military Colonization Company— failed, mostly due to the summer of neglect and partially because he suffered a broken leg which was never properly reset afterwards. This ailment caused him to walk with a pronounced limp for the rest of his life and also made riding a horse difficult. Financially, Strange was virtually destitute.

Ultimately Strange chose to leave Canada and return to England where, in a chance encounter, he met Hiram Maxim, an inventor of a "machine gun." Strange accepted Maxim's proposition for him to travel the world, promoting the gun to governments willing to watch a demonstration. He died in England on July 9, 1925, another great Canadian military hero who to this day is virtually unknown.

Strange did write an autobiography, *Gunner Jingo's Jubilee*. As with most of the artillery officers trained in England, he had received training in the art of sketching. Strange developed a reasonable competence, and his book contains several of his works of art, giving the reader a clearer insight into the events he describes.

Sergeant William Fury

This likeable, aptly named Irish member of the scouts came to Canada from Ireland as a member of the British Army. After his discharge he joined the NWMP in 1879, receiving his preliminary training at Fort Walsh. Steele respected the fiery little sergeant's similar military background, his tenacity, and courage, and they worked together for many years. He was involved in the CPR railhead strike incident, and he assisted Steele in recruiting and preparing the scouts at Calgary, using his military experience to choose "good men." Although he is rarely mentioned, he was involved in most of the incidents the scouts experienced, and was on the firing line at Frenchman Butte. Ultimately he was seriously wounded in the chest at Loon Lake and endured the bone jarring ride in the box of a confiscated wagon back to Fort Pitt. There he received additional medical attention and began to recuperate. He was transferred to North Battleford but never did recover completely, suffering from permanent lung damage as a result of the wound.

William Fury.
This post-rebellion photo was probably taken in Calgary in late 1885, prior to Fury being granted a disability pension. He never completely recovered from a chest wound suffered at Loon Lake Narrows.

In 1888, a medical recommendation was submitted on his behalf for a discharge as physically unfit for further service, with an appropriate pension being endorsed by the medical officers. In what appears to be a rare case of benevolence, the force agreed. Once released, Fury returned to Richmond Hill, Ontario, acquired a small farm, and lived there until his death on April 19, 1936. He was buried at Killean, Ontario with full RCMP honours.

Constable Peter Kerr

Kerr enlisted with the NWMP in 1882 and served under Steele on the CPR railhead during the strike, gaining valuable experience under the tutelage of Sergeant Fury. He was on the firing line at Frenchman Butte, and Loon Lake. He left the force in 1888, when his enlistment time had expired, returning back east to join the Toronto City Police. He passed away at age 81.

Constable Thomas Waring

Waring and Kerr joined the force in Southern Alberta within days of each other. Waring participated in both incidents, Frenchman Butte and Loon Lake. When his service time expired in 1887, he left the force for about six months, then re-enlisted for three more years before purchasing his discharge in 1900. He lived to the age of 85.

Constable Ralph Bell

Bell was born in England in 1861, making him 24 years old at the time of the rebellion. He was part of Steele's detachment at Beavermouth, B. C., and he returned with Sergeant Fury to Calgary to become one of the police scouts. An article in *The Saskatchewan Farmer* on December 3, 1953 located in the City of Edmonton Archives indicates he was living in good health at his home in Calgary. In the article he described the North-West Rebellion as "that racket." He also referred to Steele as "old Smooth Bore and he was a fine man." He certainly had no love for General Middleton as indicated by his perception: "There wasn't a bigger jackass in the country than Middleton and the whole thing could have been averted."

Sergeant William Parker

William Parker returned to the Fort Saskatchewan detachment, serving a total of 38 years with the NWMP, eventually retiring in Medicine Hat, Alberta. He was well-known for his storytelling, almost to the ire of listeners, who eventually dubbed him, "Bull sh— Parker"! In his defence, it must be remembered that he endured being a member of the force from the time of its inception, through to serving with Steele in the Boer War, again returning to the force until 1912! After attaining the rank of inspector he retired to enter the real estate and insurance business, which he operated until 1938. In 1931 he was listed as a member of the Board of Directors for the Canadian North-West Historical Society, an indicator that he actively participated in the preservation of western Canadian history. William Parker's life came to a close at age 92, on May 16, 1945. He is buried in a cemetery in Medicine Hat.

William Parker left a significant amount of writing for the historian to ponder. His autobiography, based on his diary as well as letters to and from his hometown in England, are collected into the book, *William Parker, Mounted Policeman*.

Reverend George McKay

At the conclusion of hostilities, Canon McKay (pronounced "McEye") returned to Fort Macleod area and ran into the same governmental bureaucratic wall that many of the others did. With considerable effort he was finally able to collect his $360 service pay. Ottawa contended he was rendering his services as a duty of his position as a clergyman, and therefore he wasn't entitled to additional compensation. A few years later, at Steele's request, he accepted a position as Indian Agent, west of Calgary. The Indians gladly endorsed this appointment as one of sensitivity to their plight. He eventually left Canada, moved to South Dakota, attained the title of archdeacon, and died at the age of 85. His end did not come at the point of a gun as might be expected of a man who, at times, lived by one.

The Fighting Preacher, the autobiography he wrote in later life, is difficult to locate. McKay was certainly one of the more "colourful" characters in western Canada's past who undeservedly rests in relative historical obscurity.

Joseph Butlin

Butlin was an original member of the NWMP, coming west with the "Great March" in 1874. He left the force and operated a stone quarry along the Elbow River near Calgary until he joined Steele's Scouts. He was with Steele in the midnight shoot-out on the Pipestone Creek, some claiming he was the marksman who shot Meminook. He returned to Calgary, and in 1901 moved to Wetaskiwin as an employee of Pat Burns, the famous Calgary rancher. He later served as Indian Agent at Hobbema for nine years. He and his wife Angelique raised ten children. He died in his late seventies, in 1930.

Thomas James "Jumbo" Fisk

Jumbo Fisk was a well-known cowboy of the Calgary area and served as a volunteer scout. He sustained a wound to the right arm when the scouts were pursuing the natives north from Frenchman Butte to Loon Lake. He lost his little finger, and the elbow joint of his right arm never regained complete mobility. Fisk became involved with a Cree woman, Rosalie New Grass, during a drinking spree in a room above a Calgary saloon. There was a violent argument between the two and Fisk beat her so severely she subsequently died. Fisk was arrested and charged with the crime but was acquitted, much to the shock of witnesses. The case was appealed by the crown and this time a "guilty" verdict was handed down on the manslaughter charge. The judge awarded a prison term of fourteen years. He served his time and was at the 1935 reunion of Steele's Scouts and present for the commemorating photograph.

North-West Rebellion Veterans.
Top row, left, is Richard Steele and Godfrey Steele next.
William Parker is in the second row, left, with large stetson hat.
Photo taken in 1925, Palliser Hotel, Calgary.

Steele's Scouts--1885 :-: :-:

Steele's Scouts Reunion, 1935.
*A few of the Calgary members of Steele's Scouts were re united
in May 1935 in Calgary. The photo and story appeared
in the* Calgary Herald *newspaper.*

Recruited by Major Sam Steele, later General Steele, the above group of Calgary's early citizens comprised the nucleus of the famous scout troop. The photograph was taken on the present site of the C.P.R. Natural Resource building. The arrow points to E. Hayes, narrator of the accompanying article. The personnel of the group includes:

Back row—William Simms, Dick Walsh, Jim "Jumbo" Fisk, Joe Butlin, Dick Broderick, Ed Hayes, Major Steele, Fred Annan and Major Hatton. Front row—Billy Scott, Joe Garreau, Tom McLellan, Bill Fielders, W. Oake, Oscar Sanson (of the *Herald* staff in 1885), C. Jardine, and "Doc" Edmonson. Immediately behind McLellan and Fielders was a scout known as "Shorty" and rated the most expert plainsman of the famous group.

APPENDIX

Steele's Scouts

Steele's Scouts was initially to be comprised of 62 men: 20 NWMP members, 20 civilian scouts, and 22 Alberta Mounted Rifles (cavalry). The complete roster was tabled and recorded in the Canadian Parliamentary Sessional Papers of 1886 (44a) dated April 19, 1886 by Mr. Sproule, MP; however, these records were lost in the parliamentary fire in 1916. Of note is the militia rank of Steele for command purposes, others retained NWMP ranks. To add to the confusion, Steele's own, official report indicates he enlisted 23 NWMP at Calgary (Parker and Chabot joined later in Edmonton) as well as other volunteers, including brothers Richard and Godfrey Steele, who acted as messengers between Major Steele and General Strange.

North West Mounted Police:

File # 3094 National Archives of Canada

Major Samuel Benfield Steele	Reg. # 3	Service: 1873-1899
Sergeant William Fury	Reg. # 333	Service: 1879-1888
Sergeant William Parker	Reg. # 28	Service: 1874-1912
Corporal Albert McDonell	Reg. # 547	Service: 1881-1917
Corporal Henry Gould	Reg. # 680	Service: 1882-1887
Corporal Alexander L. Davidson	Reg. # 523	Service: 1881-1886
Corporal W. R. McMinn	Reg. # 549	Service: 1881-1897
Constable Ralph Bell	Reg. # 590	Service: 1881-1886
Constable John Bunt	Reg. # 97	Service: 1883-1890
Constable Joseph Chabot	Reg. # 474	Service: 1880-1885
Constable Thomas Craig	Reg. # 643	Service: 1882-1890
Constable Alexander Davidson	Reg. # 648	Service: 1882-1890
Constable Oscar Duberiul	Reg. # 475	Service: 1880-1887
Constable Alexander Dyre	Reg. # 653	Service: 1882-1885
Constable Ernest Hall	Reg. # 684	Service: 1882-1886
Constable Samuel Heatherington	Reg. # 894	Service: 1883-1901
Constable George Jones	Reg. # 699	Service: 1882-1888
Constable Peter Kerr	Reg. # 704	Service: 1882-1888
Constable Donald McRae	Reg. # 716	Service: 1882-1887
Constable Robert Morton	Reg. # 719	Service: 1882-1887
Constable Ernest Percival	Reg. # 557	Service: 1881-1903
Constable Frederick Richardson	Reg. # 758	Service: 1882-1887
Constable John Robinson	Reg. # 779	Service: 1882-1887
Constable John Walters	Reg. # 795	Service: 1882-1888
Constable Thomas Waring	Reg. # 790	Service: 1882-1890
Constable James Whipps	Reg. # 784	Service: 1882-1887

Civilian Members of Steele's Scouts:

There is no way of discerning between Civilian Scouts and those who enlisted with the Alberta Mounted Rifles.

Captain J. K. Oswald In Charge under Commanding Officer Major Steele

Calgary Inductees

William Fielders
Edward F. Racey
R. L. Barber
George Borradaille
William Simms
William Scott
Joseph Garand
Richard Broderick
John Corryell
John Alley
Thomas Anderson
Joseph Benoit
Joseph Garand
Watson Hunt
William Huston
William Jardine
William Lyne
Frank Miller
William McQuarrie
Donald Macpherson
Frank Owen
Arthur Philipps
James Rogers
Albert Simons
Reverend John McDougall
William Inglis
James Rogers

Thomas James "Jumbo" Fisk
William West
? Nash
Milton Williams
Albert Welsh
Peter Young
William Oake
Edward Hayes
Frederick Annan
William Fisk
Linas Ahlenius
Edward Cole
George Gouin
Charles Hurrell
Frank Owen
Samuel Kendig
William Murray
William McManus
Robert McFarlane
William McKellar
W. F. Pew
William Jardine
Alexander Smith
Louis Trepanier
Joseph Butlin
Charles Sanson
Harry Smith

Edmonton Inductees

Reverend George McKay chaplin (enroute)
William Ibbleson
Wyndham Spearin
William West
J. Calder
John Beldon
Alexander Rowland
"Doc" Thomas Edmonson
C. Whitford
John Whitford
B. Laroque

James Petrie
Frederick Walters
Arthur Patton
Walter Rowland
Fred Rowland
George White
A. B. Spence
L. Whitford
William Stiff

CHRONOLOGY

July 8, 1874	North West Mounted Police commence "Great March" west from Fort Dufferin to Fort Macleod.
August 23, 1876	Sam Steele at the signing of Treaty Number Six outside Fort Carlton.
September 9, 1876	Sam Steele at the signing of Treaty Number Six outside Fort Pitt.
June 5, 1884	Louis Riel agrees to return to Saskatchewan from exile in Montana.
March 19, 1885	Louis Riel declares a provisional government at Batoche, Saskatchewan.
March 26, 1885	Major Leif Crozier's NWMP and volunteers are defeated at Duck Lake.
March 29, 1885	A.P. Caron, Minister of Militia, requests retired General Thomas B. Strange to form the Alberta Field Force at Calgary
April 2,1885	Wandering Spirit initiates the massacre of nine men at Frog Lake.
April 11, 1885	Sam Steele arrives in Calgary, and meets with General Strange who orders formation of Steele's Scouts.
April 12, 1885	General Strange receives approval for Sam Steele to command his scouts.
April 13, 1885	A large Cree force surrounds Fort Pitt.
April 15, 1885	Inspector Francis Dickens abandons Fort Pitt to float down the North Saskatchewan River to Battleford. Civilians become hostages of the Cree under War Chief Wandering Spirit.

April 20, 1885	Steele's Scouts lead the Alberta Field Force out of Calgary to Edmonton.
April 25, 1885	General Middleton's militia and Gabriel Dumont's Métis force meet in battle at Fish Creek.
May 1, 1885	Steele's Scouts, leading the Alberta Field Force, arrives in Edmonton.
May 3, 1885	Colonel Otter's force attacks Chief Poundmaker's camp at Cutknife Hill and is badly mauled by the defending Cree warriors.
May 6, 1885	Steele's Scouts move out of Edmonton, marching downriver to Victoria.
May 9, 1885	General Middleton's militia arrive at Batoche and commence a siege.
May 12, 1885	Batoche falls to Middleton's force after an impromptu charge by soldiers.
May 15, 1885	Louis Riel surrenders to General Middleton.
May 17, 1885	Steele's Scouts depart from Victoria, heading east.
May 24, 1885	The 65th Mount Royal Rifles erect a commemorative cross above the mouth of Frog Creek on the North Saskatchewan River.
May 26, 1885	Sam Steele and his scouts confront Cree men in a midnight gunfight.
May 28, 1885	General Strange's Alberta Field Force confronts Wandering Spirit's Cree in Battle of Frenchman Butte.
June 2, 1885	Sam Steele leads 63 men in pursuit of the Cree fleeing toward Loon Lake.
June 3,1885	Steele's Scouts attack the Cree in an attempt to free the hostages at Loon Lake Narrows. Battle ends inconclusively and Steele withdraws.
June 4, 1885	Steele's Scouts meet up with General Middleton's cavalry then continue the pursuit of the Cree.

June 9, 1885	General Middleton orders a withdrawal of the force back to Fort Pitt.
June 14, 1885	Steele's Scouts and part of Middleton's force arrive at Cold Lake.
June 17, 1885	Steele's Scouts return to Fort Pitt.
June 18, 1885	Word received in Fort Pitt that the captives have been freed.
July 2, 1885	Cree Chief Big Bear voluntarily surrenders.
July 3, 1885	Sam Steele and civilian members of the scouts depart Fort Pitt, returning to Edmonton.
July 18, 1885	Sam Steele and his scouts enter Calgary, home at last.
November 16, 1885	Louis Riel is hanged in Regina.
November 27, 1885	Wandering Spirit and five other Cree warriors are hanged at Battleford.

ENDNOTES

Prologue
1. Gage Canadian Dictionary.
2. The Fenians were Irish immigrants in the United States who tried to support an Irish revolutionary group in England by making several armed raids into the colony of Canada prior to Confederation.

Chapter One
3. This document is on display in the RCMP museum in Regina.
4. Inspector Dickens (son of novelist Charles Dickens) appointed the adult residents of Fort Pitt as "ex-officio" members of the NWMP so he could issue police firearms to them. One of those appointed and issued a rifle was Amelia McLean (age 18), daughter of chief trader W.J. McLean. It appears Amelia was the first to open fire with her rifle from the barricades in a desperate attempt to protect the wounded Constable Loasby staggering toward the safety of the fort. Technically, she is likely the first female member of the NWMP or RCMP.

Chapter Two
5. Kootenai Brown, one of the last true "mountain men," led an extremely colourful life and resided on the shores of Waterton Lake. Through his diligent effort it is today the site of a National Park.
6. Some of the police who were not scouts, such as the gun team for the cannon from Fort Macleod, retained their scarlet tunics during the campaign.

Chapter Four
7. One of the police members killed was Constable Sleigh from Fort Pitt, enticed into raising his head to look at an Indian waving a blanket. The Indian snipers worked in a team, one safely making a visible movement, while the other picked off anyone who showed himself.

8. Poundmaker, Chief. *Chief Poundmaker Historic Centre, Cutknife Hill, SK.*
9. Personal letter to his sister, Glenbow Archives, Calgary, AB.
10. Ibid.
11. Strange, Thomas Bland. *Gunner Jingo's Jubilee.*
12. McKay, Archdeacon George. *The Fighting Parson.*
13. Strange, Thomas Bland. *Gunner Jingo's Jubilee.*
14. Ibid.
15. Chambers, Captain Ernest J. *History of the 65th Mount Royal Rifles in Western Canada.*

Chapter Five
16. Cameron, William Bleasdell. *Blood Red The Sun.*
17. Ibid.
18. Dunn, Jack. *The Alberta Field Force, 1885.*
19. MacBeth, Reverend R.G. *The Making of the Canadian West.*
20. Chambers, Captain Ernest J. *History of the 65th Mount Royal Rifles in Western Canada.*

Chapter Seven
21. MacBeth, Reverend R.G. *The Making of the Canadian West.*
22. McLean, Duncan. *Weekend Magazine #33,* 1968.
23. McKay, Archdeacon George. *The Fighting Parson.*

Chapter Eight
24. The next year at Fort Belknap in the U.S.A., White Poplar was killed during an altercation with an unknown Métis man.
25. Macleod, R.C. *Reminiscences of a Bungle.*
26. Ibid.
27. Middleton, General Sir Frederick. *Suppression of the Rebellion in the North West Territories.*

Chapter Nine
28. Roy R.H. *Rifleman Florin in the Riel Rebellion.*
29. A 30-metre-distant target is exceedingly long for a handgun of the type issued to the NWMP. Luck must have played a significant role or the described range was misjudged.
30. The executed natives have not been completely forgotten as the author has noted small remembrances placed on their common grave from time to time.

BIBLIOGRAPHY

Cameron, William Bleasdell. *Blood Red The Sun.* Calgary, AB: Kenway Publishing Co., 1926.

Canadian North-West Historical Society. *The Alberta Field Force of 1885.* North Battleford, SK: Canadian North-West Historical Society Publication, 1931.

Dempsey, Hugh. *Calgary, Spirit of the West.* Calgary, AB: Fifth House Publishing Ltd.,1994.

Dempsey, Hugh H. *William Parker, Mounted Policeman.* Edmonton, AB: Glenbow Insitute; Hurtig Publishers, 1973.

Dunn, Jack. *The Alberta Field Force.* Calgary, AB: Jack Dunn, 1994.

Erasmus, Peter. *Buffalo Days and Nights.* Calgary, AB: Fifth House Publishing Ltd., 1999.

Fort Pitt Historical Society. *Fort Pitt History Unfolding.* Fort Pitt, SK: 1985.

Hughes, Stuart. *The Frog Lake "Massacre."* Toronto, ON: McClelland & Stewart Ltd., 1976.

Kelly, Nora and William. *The Royal Canadian Mounted Police.* Edmonton, AB: Hurtig Publishers, 1973.

Klancher, Donald. *The N.W.M.P. and the Northwest Rebellion.* Kamloops, BC: Mounted Police Research and Consulting, 1997.

Light, Douglas W. *Footprints in the Dust.* North Battleford, SK: Turner-Warwick Publications Inc., 1987

Loew, Franklin & Edward Wood. *Vet in the Saddle.* Saskatoon, SK: Western Producer Prairie Books, 1978.

MacBeth, Reverend R.G. *The Making of the Canadian West.* Toronto, ON: William Biggs,1898.

Macleod, R. C. *Reminiscences of a Bungle.* Edmonton, AB: University of Alberta Press, 1983.

McKay, Archdeacon George. *Fighting Parson.* Kelowna, BC: M.E. McKay, 1931.

Middleton, General Sir Frederick. *Suppression of the Rebellion in the North West Territories.* Toronto, ON: University of Toronto Press, 1948.

Residents. *At Our Crossing, A Local History of Brosseau and Area.* Edmonton, AB: Co-op Press Ltd., 1980.

Saul, Donovan T. *Red Serge and Stetsons.* Victoria, BC: Horsdal & Schubart Publishers Ltd., 1993.

Steele, Samuel B. *Forty Years In Canada.* New York, NY: Dodd, Mead, 1915.

Stewart, Robert. *Sam Steele, Lion of the Frontier.* Toronto, ON: Doubleday & Co. Inc., 1979.

Stonechild, Blair and Bill Waiser. *Loyal Till Death.* Calgary AB: Fifth House Ltd., 1997.

Strange, Thomas Bland. *Gunner Jingo's Jubilee.* Edmonton, AB: The University Of Alberta Press, 1988.

Wallace, Jim. *A Trying Time.* Winnipeg, MB: Bunker to Bunker Books, 1998.

Periodicals and Other Sources

Chambers, Captain Ernest J. *History of the 65th Mount Royal Rifles in Western Canada.* French language report, 1906; translation D. Fleshman, 1992.

Historical Society of Alberta. *Alberta Field Force.* Edmonton, AB: Autumn 1978.

Middleton, General Sir Frederick. Report of Operations of Alberta Field Force.1885.

Province of Saskatchewan. *A Saskatchewan Historic Site: STEELE NARROWS.* Saskatchewan Diamond Jubilee & Canada Centennial Corporation, 1965.

Roy, R.H. *Rifleman Florin In The Riel Rebellion.* Saskatchewan History, Province of Saskatchewan Archives Board, 1948.

Steele, James Bond. *Personal Diary and letters.* Alberta Provincial Archives, 1885.

Wells, Eric. *The last hostage.* Weekend Magazine #33, Edmonton Archives, 1968.

Williams, Milton. *Letter to his sister.* Glenbow Archives, 28/06/1895.

INDEX

PHOTO CREDITS

Archives of Saskatchewan: A-6276 (p. 153).

Calgary Public Library: (p. 173).

Donald Klancher: (p. 109; p. 169).

Glenbow Archives: NA-1825-6 (p. 17), NA-2446-8 (p. 21), NA-294-1 (p. 25), NA-967-12 (p. 26), NA-936-22 (p. 32), NA-660-1 (p. 33), NA-670-53 (p. 34), NA-1193-9 (p. 35), NA-1323 4 (p. 35), NA-1847-2 (p. 44), P-1390-50 (p. 45), NA-2514-1 (p. 53), NA-18-3 (p. 54), NA-1351-1 (p. 61), NA-1817-3 (p. 65), NA-216-4 (p. 68), P-1390-30 (p. 75), P-1390-44 (p. 78), NA-1817-4 (p. 92), NA-1193-1 (p. 94), NA-1817-5 (p. 106), P-1390-44 (p. 107), NA-2381-1 (p. 113), NA-1353-32 (p. 115), P-1390-2 (p. 138), NA-1032-3 (p. 140), P-1390-55 (p. 142), P-1390-16 (p. 143), NA-363-66 (p. 144), P-1390-5-1 (p. 150), NA-1480-37 (p. 150), P-1390-27 (p. 151), NA-1480-34 (p. 152), NA-1480-38 (p. 153), NA-1036-1 (p. 156), NA-1406-137 (p. 158), NA-1753-52 (p. 161), NA-2382-1 (p. 163), NA-2883-24 (p. 169); NA-8-385 (p. 172).

National Archives of Canada: PA 204294 (p. 22), B-2199 (p. 141), B-2072 (p. 144), PA-865-63 (p. 149), C-595 (p. 155), PA-28894 (p. 165), PA-201377 (p. 166).

Provincial Archives of Alberta: A-1821 (p. 20), B-2012 (p. 51), P-3443 (p. 63), B-9936 (p. 65), B-2406 (p. 69), B-1056 (p. 73), A-1461 (p. 74), B-1689 (p. 88), B-1968 (p. 167), PA-5911 (p. 167 bottom).

Saskatchewan Archives Board: R-A27292 (p. 112), R-A9213 (p. 123), R-A8812 (p. 154).

The remainder of the photos have been provided by the author.